OFFICIAL SQA PAST PAPERS WITH ANSWERS

STANDARD GRADE | GENERAL | CREDIT

GERMAN 2007-2011

2007 GENERAL LEVEL – page 3
2007 General Level Reading – 2007 General Level Listening Transcript – 2007 General Level Listening

2007 CREDIT LEVEL – page 25
2007 Credit Level Reading – 2007 Credit Level Listening Transcript – 2007 Credit Level Listening

2008 GENERAL LEVEL – page 43
2008 General Level Reading – 2008 General Level Listening Transcript – 2008 General Level Listening

2008 CREDIT LEVEL – page 65
2008 Credit Level Reading – 2008 Credit Level Listening Transcript – 2008 Credit Level Listening

2009 GENERAL LEVEL – page 83
2009 General Level Reading – 2009 General Level Listening Transcript – 2009 General Level Listening

2009 CREDIT LEVEL – page 107
2009 Credit Level Reading – 2009 Credit Level Listening Transcript – 2009 Credit Level Listening

2010 GENERAL LEVEL – page 129
2010 General Level Reading – 2010 General Level Listening Transcript – 2010 General Level Listening

2010 CREDIT LEVEL – page 151
2010 Credit Level Reading – 2010 Credit Level Listening Transcript – 2010 Credit Level Listening

2011 GENERAL LEVEL – page 171
2011 General Level Reading – 2011 General Level Listening Transcript – 2011 General Level Listening

2011 CREDIT LEVEL – page 193
2011 Credit Level Reading – 2011 Credit Level Listening Transcript – 2011 Credit Level Listening

ANSWER SECTION – page 215

Publisher's Note

We are delighted to bring you the 2011 Past Papers and you will see that we have changed the format from previous editions. As part of our environmental awareness strategy, we have attempted to make these new editions as sustainable as possible.
To do this, we have printed on white paper and bound the answer sections into the book. This not only allows us to use significantly less paper but we are also, for the first time, able to source all the materials from sustainable sources.

We hope you like the new editions and by purchasing this product, you are not only supporting an independent Scottish publishing company but you are also, in the International Year of Forests, not contributing to the destruction of the world's forests.

Thank you for your support and please see the following websites for more information to support the above statement –

www.fsc-uk.org

www.loveforests.com

First exam published in 2007.
Published by Bright Red Publishing Ltd, 6 Stafford Street, Edinburgh EH3 7AU
tel: 0131 220 5804 fax: 0131 220 6710 info@brightredpublishing.co.uk www.brightredpublishing.co.uk

ISBN 978-1-84948-171-7

A CIP Catalogue record for this book is available from the British Library.

Bright Red Publishing is grateful to the copyright holders, as credited on the final page of the Question Section, for permission to use their material. Every effort has been made to trace the copyright holders and to obtain their permission for the use of copyright material. Bright Red Publishing will be happy to receive information allowing us to rectify any error or omission in future editions.

STANDARD GRADE | GENERAL

2007

[BLANK PAGE]

FOR OFFICIAL USE

G

Total

1300/402

NATIONAL QUALIFICATIONS 2007

FRIDAY, 25 MAY
10.05 AM – 10.50 AM

GERMAN STANDARD GRADE
General Level
Reading

Fill in these boxes and read what is printed below.

Full name of centre

Town

Forename(s)

Surname

Date of birth
Day Month Year

Scottish candidate number

Number of seat

When you are told to do so, open your paper and write your answers **in English** in the spaces provided.

You may use a German dictionary.

Before leaving the examination room you must give this book to the invigilator. If you do not, you may lose all the marks for this paper.

SCOTTISH QUALIFICATIONS AUTHORITY

DO NOT WRITE IN THIS MARGIN

Marks

You are spending a week in Germany with your pen friend.

1. You look at the headlines in a newspaper.

A	**Leichtathletik : Weltrekord im Waldstadion**
B	**Ferienbeginn — Chaos auf der Autobahn**
C	**Polizistin verhaftet zwei Verbrecher im Einkaufszentrum**
D	**Neue Ausstellung — Tausende von Touristen in der Staatsgalerie**
E	**Englischer Außenminister und amerikanischer Vizepräsident zu Gast im Rathaus**

Match the German headlines above to the English versions below.

Write the correct letter in each box. **4**

	Letter
Holiday traffic causes problems	
Foreign politicians visit German town	
New exhibition is a hit	
World record broken	
Criminals arrested	

DO NOT WRITE IN THIS MARGIN

Marks

2. In this article, people say what they would do if they won the lottery.

What would they do? Write the correct name in the grid below. **3**

Who would . . .

	Name
. . . have a long lie every day?	
. . . build a house in the country?	
. . . buy a car?	
. . . go on holiday?	

DO NOT WRITE IN THIS MARGIN

Marks

3. In this article, young people write about truanting from school.

Ich schwänze immer, weil ich keine Freunde in meiner Klasse habe. Meine Mutter arbeitet ganztags, und ich sitze immer im Haus und sehe fern.

Julia (13)

Meine Noten sind immer schlecht, und ich habe keine Lust, in die Schule zu gehen. Ich treffe ein paar Freunde in der Stadt, und wir verbringen den ganzen Tag in der Fußgängerzone.

Arno (15)

Ich schwänze seit ein paar Monaten. Mein Geschichtslehrer ist einfach zu streng, und ich habe Angst vor ihm. Statt in die Schule zu gehen, gehe ich zum Hafen und sehe mir die Schiffe an.

Michael (14)

Why do they truant and what do they do instead of going to school?

Fill in the grid below. **6**

	Why they truant	**What they do instead**
Julia		
Arno		
Michael		

DO NOT WRITE IN THIS MARGIN

Marks

4. These people write about why they feel discriminated against.

Ich möchte einen kleinen Nebenjob finden, aber das ist sehr schwierig, weil ich Rentner bin.

Manfred

Ich bin Rollstuhlfahrer, und es ärgert mich, dass es in der Bibliothek keinen Fahrstuhl gibt.

Peter

Ich fühle mich diskriminiert. Ich darf in der Fußballmannschaft in meiner Schule nicht mitspielen, weil ich ein Mädchen bin.

Theresa

Ich habe manchmal Probleme, weil ich hier als Ausländer angesehen werde. Ich komme aus Italien, und manche Leute halten mich für doof, weil meine Deutschkenntnisse nicht perfekt sind.

Maria

Write the correct name in each box. **3**

Who feels discriminated against because of . . .

	Name
. . . their nationality?	
. . . their sex?	
. . . their age?	
. . . a lack of disabled access?	

[Turn over

Marks

5. These young people write about how they plan to celebrate their birthday.

Ich will mit meinen Freunden in die Kegelbahn gehen. Sie organisieren alles: Einladungen, das Essen usw.

Gabi

Ich werde mit den Eltern zu Hause feiern. Ich will Geld für den Urlaub im Sommer sparen.

Tina

Ich werde meine Lieblingsband im Liveauftritt sehen. Meine Mutter hat die Karten in einem Wettbewerb gewonnen.

Tom

Ich möchte mit Freunden Quadbikes mieten. Das finde ich wirklich aufregend.

Lars

(*a*) What type of party do **Gabi** and **Tina** want? Write the correct name below each picture. **1**

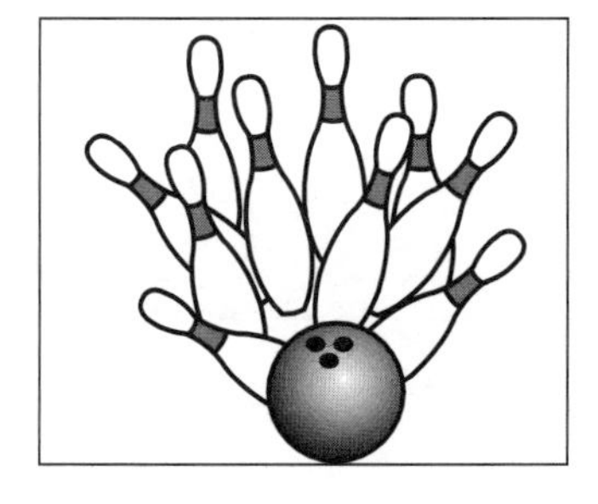

(*b*) How did Tom get tickets to see his favourite band in concert? **1**

____

(*c*) Why does Lars want to hire quad bikes? **1**

____

[Turn over for Question 6 on *Page eight*

DO NOT WRITE IN THIS MARGIN

Marks

6. These German students write about how they earn money.

Ich bin Studentin in Heidelberg und muss an zwei Tagen in der Woche arbeiten. Ich verkaufe Blumen am Markt und so habe ich immer die Gelegenheit, mit Touristen aus anderen Ländern in Kontakt zu kommen. Das ist sehr praktisch, weil ich Fremdsprachen studiere.

Lara (20)

Ich bin Sportstudent in Göttingen und ich arbeite am Abend im Hallenbad. Ich gebe Schwimmstunden und ich habe viel über die Arbeit mit Jugendlichen gelernt. Das ist sehr hilfreich, denn ich möchte später Sportlehrer werden.

Thomas (23)

Ich habe normalerweise keine Zeit und ich arbeite nur in den Ferien. Dann habe ich einen kleinen Nebenjob im Stadttheater, wo ich Programmhefte verkaufe. Das ist für mich sehr interessant, denn ich möchte später Schauspielerin werden.

Jelena (21)

(*a*) Write the correct name in each box. **2**

Who works . . .

	Name
. . . in the holidays only?	
. . . two days a week?	
. . . in the evenings?	

DO NOT WRITE IN THIS MARGIN

Marks

6. (continued)

(*b*) What do they do and how will their jobs help them in their future careers?

Fill in the grid below. **6**

Name	**Works at**	**What they do there**	**How the job will help in their future career**
Lara	Market		
Thomas	Swimming pool		
Jelena	Theatre		

[Turn over for Question 7 on *Page ten*

Marks

7. German rock star Max Haller is interviewed about looking good and staying healthy.

- *Max, ist dir das Aussehen wichtig?*

Ja, natürlich. Ich gehe regelmäßig zum Friseur. Ich versuche immer gesunde Sachen zu essen, und so kann ich auf die Figur achten.

- *Hast du ein paar Tipps für unsere Leser?*

Ich habe drei goldene Gesundheitsregeln:

- **Niemals rauchen.**
- **Mindestens dreimal in der Woche Sport treiben.**
- **Versuche immer acht Stunden am Tag zu schlafen.**

(*a*) How does Max keep himself looking good? Write **two** things. **2**

____

____

____

(*b*) Max has three golden rules for good health.

What are they? Complete the sentences. **3**

Never ______________________________.

You should do sport ______________________________.

Always try to ______________________________.

Total (32)

[*END OF QUESTION PAPER*]

G

1300/407

NATIONAL QUALIFICATIONS 2007

FRIDAY, 25 MAY
1.45 PM – 2.10 PM
(APPROX)

GERMAN
STANDARD GRADE
General Level
Listening Transcript

This paper must not be seen by any candidate.

The material overleaf is provided for use in an emergency only (eg the recording or equipment proving faulty) or where permission has been given in advance by SQA for the material to be read to candidates with additional support needs. The material must be read exactly as printed.

Transcript—General Level

Instructions to reader(s):

For each item, read the English **once,** then read the German **three times**, with an interval of 5 seconds between the readings. On completion of the third reading, pause for the length of time indicated in brackets after each item, to allow the candidates to write their answers.

Where special arrangements have been agreed in advance to allow the reading of the material, those sections marked **(f)** should be read by a female speaker and those marked **(m)** by a male: those sections marked **(t)** should be read by the teacher.

(t) You are going to Germany to spend a week with your pen friend, Martin.

(f) or (m) **Du fährst nach Deutschland, um eine Woche bei deinem Brieffreund, Martin, zu verbringen.**

(t) Question number one.

When you arrive at the house, Martin offers you breakfast.

What does he offer you? Tick the correct box.

(m) **Zum Frühstück essen wir normalerweise Brot mit Käse und verschiedenen Wurstsorten. Dazu trinken wir Kaffee. Schmeckt dir das?**

(30 seconds)

(t) Question number two.

Martin shows you to your room.

Where is your room? Tick the correct box.

(m) **Dein Zimmer ist im ersten Stock neben meinem Zimmer. Das Badezimmer ist deinem Zimmer gegenüber.**

(30 seconds)

(t) Question number three.

Martin shares a room with his younger brother.

Why does he not like this? Write **two** things.

(m) **Ich teile ein Zimmer mit meinem jüngeren Bruder. Er hört laute Musik, wenn ich meine Hausaufgaben mache, und ich kann mich nicht konzentrieren. Und er nimmt oft meine Sachen—meine Bücher und CDs usw.**

(30 seconds)

(t) Question number four.

Martin talks about his school timetable.

Which subjects does he have tomorrow? Write the correct subjects in the grid.

(m) **Morgen in der ersten Stunde habe ich Chemie bei Frau Schneider. In der zweiten Stunde habe ich Erdkunde bei Herrn Braun. Das finde ich toll.**

(30 seconds)

(t) Question number five.

Martin's mother asks you about school.

What does she ask? Tick **three** boxes.

(f) **Ich möchte etwas über die Schule in Schottland erfahren. Wie lange dauert eine Stunde in deiner Schule? Was machst du in der Pause? Wie findest du Deutsch?**

(30 seconds)

(t) Question number six.

Martin tells you that he looks forward to Fridays.

Why is this? Write **two** things.

(m) **Ich freue mich immer auf Freitag. Wir haben nur fünf Stunden in der Schule und sind schon um zwölf Uhr fertig. Nachmittags gehe ich mit Freunden in die Stadt. Das macht großen Spaß.**

(30 seconds)

(t) Question number seven.

Martin's mother talks about mealtimes.

How are Friday evenings different from other evenings? Write **two** things.

(f) **Normalerweise koche ich das Abendessen, aber am Freitag kochen Martin und seine Brüder. Freitags essen wir nicht im Esszimmer, sondern wir essen vor dem Fernseher im Wohnzimmer.**

(30 seconds)

(t) Question number eight.

Martin's mother talks about the weekend.

What will the weather be like? What does she suggest you could do? Write **two** things.

(f) **Am Wochenende soll es regnerisch und ziemlich kalt sein. Ihr könntet entweder in die Eishalle gehen oder das Stadtmuseum besuchen. Oder würdest du lieber deine Postkarten schreiben?**

(30 seconds)

(t) Question number nine.

Martin's mother tells you that her eldest son, Sebastian, is a computer programmer.

What are the advantages of his job? Tick **two** boxes.

What is the disadvantage?

(f) **Sebastian arbeitet als Programmierer. Der Job ist gut bezahlt. Er fährt oft ins Ausland. Erst letzte Woche war er in Spanien. Leider muss er oft nachts arbeiten und das findet er natürlich nicht so gut.**

(30 seconds)

[Turn over for Questions 10, 11, 12 and 13 on *Page four*

(t) Question number ten.

Martin would like to work with computers too.

Why would this type of work suit him? Write **two** things.

(m) **Ich möchte auch in der Computerbranche arbeiten. Ich habe viele gute Ideen für neue Spiele und ich schreibe Artikel über Computer für die Schülerzeitung.**

(30 seconds)

(t) Question number eleven.

Martin's mother talks about problems with working with computers.

What does she say? Write **one** thing.

(f) **In diesem Beruf muss man stundenlang vor dem Computer sitzen. Das ist ungesund und nicht gut für die Augen.**

(30 seconds)

(t) Question number twelve.

You are going to visit Martin's friend, Petra. His mother tells you where she lives.

Are the following statements **True** or **False**? Tick the correct box for each one.

(f) **Petras Familie hat eine neue Wohnung am Stadtrand. Da die Wohnung im vierten Stock ist, haben sie keinen Garten.**

(30 seconds)

(t) Question number thirteen.

Martin tells you that he gets on well with Petra.

Why is this? Complete the sentence.

(m) **Ich komme gut mit Petra aus. Sie ist sehr lustig. Wir haben den gleichen Geschmack, was Mode betrifft.**

(30 seconds)

(t) End of test.

Now look over your answers.

[*END OF TRANSCRIPT*]

FOR OFFICIAL USE

G

Total Mark

1300/406

NATIONAL QUALIFICATIONS 2007

FRIDAY, 25 MAY
1.45 PM – 2.10 PM (APPROX)

GERMAN
STANDARD GRADE
General Level
Listening

Fill in these boxes and read what is printed below.

Full name of centre

Town

Forename(s)

Surname

Date of birth
Day Month Year

Scottish candidate number

Number of seat

When you are told to do so, open your paper.

You will hear a number of short items in German. You will hear each item three times, then you will have time to write your answer.

Write your answers, **in English**, in this book, in the appropriate spaces.

You may take notes as you are listening to the German, but only in this paper.

You may **not** use a German dictionary.

You are not allowed to leave the examination room until the end of the test.

Before leaving the examination room you must give this book to the invigilator. If you do not, you may lose all the marks for this paper.

Marks

You are going to Germany to spend a week with your pen friend, Martin.

Du fährst nach Deutschland, um eine Woche bei deinem Brieffreund, Martin, zu verbringen.

1. When you arrive at the house, Martin offers you breakfast.

What does he offer you? Tick (✓) the correct box. **1**

☐ ☐ ☐

* * * * *

2. Martin shows you to your room.

Where is your room? Tick (✓) the correct box. **1**

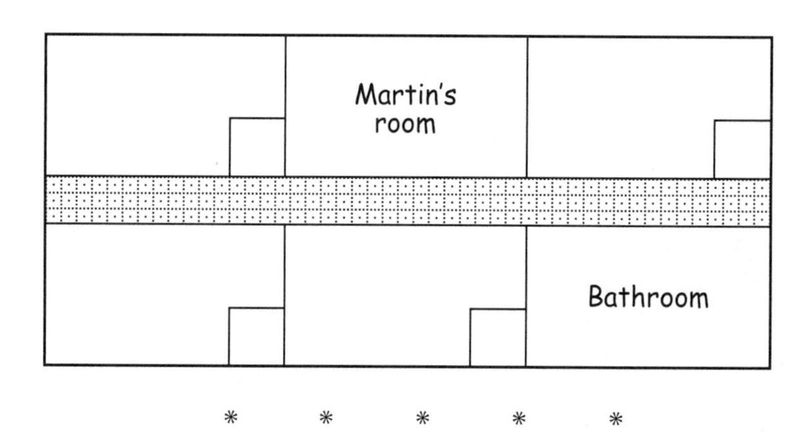

* * * * *

3. Martin shares a room with his younger brother.

Why does he not like this? Write **two** things. **2**

____

____

____

* * * * *

DO NOT WRITE IN THIS MARGIN

Marks

4. Martin talks about his school timetable.

Which subjects does he have tomorrow? Write the correct subjects in the grid. **2**

	Subject
1st lesson	
2nd lesson	

* * * * *

5. Martin's mother asks you about school.

What does she ask? Tick (✓) **three** boxes. **3**

	Tick (✓)
How many lessons do you have each day?	
How long does each lesson last?	
When is break time?	
What do you do at break time?	
What do you think of German?	
Do you have to learn German?	

* * * * *

6. Martin tells you that he looks forward to Fridays.

Why is this? Write **two** things. **2**

____

____

____

* * * * *

[Turn over

Marks

7. Martin's mother talks about mealtimes.

How are Friday evenings different from other evenings? Write **two** things. **2**

* * * * *

8. Martin's mother talks about the weekend.

(*a*) What will the weather be like? **1**

(*b*) What does she suggest you could do? Write **two** things. **2**

* * * * *

9. Martin's mother tells you that her eldest son, Sebastian, is a computer programmer.

(*a*) What are the advantages of his job? Tick (✓) **two** boxes. **2**

	Tick (✓)
Good pay	
Long holidays	
Travelling abroad	
Company car	
Friendly colleagues	

(*b*) What is the disadvantage? **1**

* * * * *

DO NOT WRITE IN THIS MARGIN

Marks

10. Martin would like to work with computers too.

Why would this type of work suit him? Write **two** things. 2

____

____

____

* * * * *

11. Martin's mother talks about problems with working with computers.

What does she say? Write **one** thing. 1

____

____

* * * * *

12. You are going to visit Martin's friend, Petra. His mother tells you where she lives.

Are the following statements **True** or **False**? Tick (✓) the correct box for each one. 2

	True	**False**
Petra's family lives in the town centre.		
They have a garden.		

* * * * *

13. Martin tells you that he gets on well with Petra.

Why is this? Complete the sentence. 2

Petra is very ____________________ and they share the same taste

in ____________________ .

* * * * *

Total (26)

[*END OF QUESTION PAPER*]

[BLANK PAGE]

STANDARD GRADE | CREDIT

2007

[BLANK PAGE]

FOR OFFICIAL USE

C

Total

1300/403

NATIONAL QUALIFICATIONS 2007

FRIDAY, 25 MAY
11.10 AM – 12.10 PM

GERMAN
STANDARD GRADE
Credit Level
Reading

Fill in these boxes and read what is printed below.

Full name of centre

Town

Forename(s)

Surname

Date of birth
Day Month Year

Scottish candidate number

Number of seat

When you are told to do so, open your paper and write your answers **in English** in the spaces provided.

You may use a German dictionary.

Before leaving the examination room you must give this book to the invigilator. If you do not, you may lose all the marks for this paper.

SCOTTISH QUALIFICATIONS AUTHORITY

DO NOT WRITE IN THIS MARGIN

Marks

1. More and more Germans are thinking about a career change these days.

Geld regiert die Welt—das haben wir alle schon als Kinder gelernt. Die Finanzen sind aber nicht immer der wichtigste Grund, wenn es um die Motivation für einen Jobwechsel geht. Für viele Arbeiter in Deutschland ist es wichtiger, dass der künftige Job eine neue Herausforderung bedeutet. Andere wünschen sich mehr Freizeit, und viele Leute wollen in eine neue Gegend oder in eine neue Stadt umziehen.

(*a*) **Apart from money**, what reasons do Germans give for wanting a career change? Write **two** things. **2**

____

____

____

Jens, a 28-year-old German, writes about his experience of changing career.

Als ich meinen neuen Job bekam, war ich wirklich erleichtert. Ich war schon drei Monate lang arbeitslos gewesen, und meine Frau hatte nur einen kleinen Nebenjob, weil wir zwei junge Kinder haben.

Dann kam meine erste Woche im Büro. Ich habe mein ganzes Leben nur mit den Händen gearbeitet, und ich war wirklich erstaunt, wie anstrengend es ist, sieben Stunden am Tag Namen und Adressen in den Computer zu geben. Briefumschläge habe ich auch gestopft. Nach drei Wochen wurde ich sehr deprimiert, ich hatte keine Lust mehr, aus dem Haus zu gehen, und mein Familienleben begann darunter zu leiden.

(*b*) Why was Jens so relieved when he got his new job? Write **two** things. **2**

____

____

____

(*c*) What surprised him about working in an office? **1**

____

____

DO NOT WRITE IN THIS MARGIN

1. (continued) *Marks*

(*d*) What negative effects did his job have on him? Write **two** things. **2**

____

____

____

[Turn over

DO NOT WRITE IN THIS MARGIN

Marks

2. Kenny, a Scottish boy, decided to go to university in Germany when he left school. He writes about his experiences.

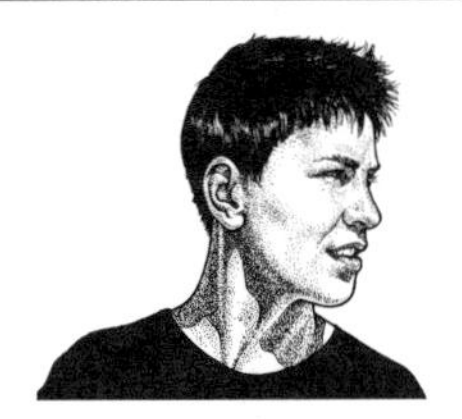

Ich bin in Dundee geboren und aufgewachsen, aber sobald ich mit der Schule fertig war, beschloss ich in Deutschland zu studieren. Erstens bin ich zweisprachig—meine Mutter ist Deutsche. Zweitens wollte ich Chemie mit Sport studieren, und das kann man bei uns in Schottland nicht. Ich habe Verwandte in Heidelberg, einer Stadt mit einer sehr alten, berühmten Universität, und zum Glück hatten sie ein freies Zimmer.

(*a*) Why did Kenny decide to go and study in Germany? Write **three** things. **3**

____

____

____

____

Am Anfang waren meine Eltern mit meiner Idee gar nicht einverstanden. „Die deutschen Schüler sind an ein anderes Schulsystem gewöhnt", sagte mein Vater. „Die Schüler in Deutschland sind oft ein paar Jahre älter, wenn sie das Studium beginnen, und das macht schon einen großen Unterschied."

Meine Mutter sah ein anderes Problem: „Deine Tante wird sich um dich kümmern, aber du wirst vielleicht Heimweh haben. Das macht mir Sorgen."

(*b*) What things did Kenny's father think would make life difficult for him in Germany? Write **two** things. **2**

____

____

____

(*c*) What concerned his mother? **1**

____

____

DO NOT WRITE IN THIS MARGIN

2. (continued) *Marks*

Das Studentenleben war ziemlich lustig, wenn auch etwas teurer, als ich erwartet hatte. Vor meiner Ankunft in Deutschland hatte ich nie gelernt, wie man mit Geld umgeht—ich war immer nur zu meinen Eltern gegangen, wenn ich etwas brauchte. Jetzt in Deutschland bekam ich das Geld jeden Monat von meinen Eltern auf mein Bankkonto überwiesen und ich musste lernen, wie man für einen ganzen Monat planen soll. Das war am Anfang sehr schwierig für mich.

(*d*) Why did Kenny's previous experience with money make it hard for him to cope when he arrived in Germany? Write **two** things. **2**

____

____

____

(*e*) How did he get money in Germany? **1**

____

____

(*f*) What did he have to learn to do? **1**

____

____

[Turn over

Marks

3. Ursula, a Swiss girl, writes about her experience of anti-poverty demonstrations in Edinburgh.

Als die erste Demonstration stattfand, war ich schon seit zwei Wochen in Edinburg. Ich war eigentlich da, um ein dreiwöchiges Arbeitspraktikum in einem Altersheim zu machen. Meine Gastfamilie wollte an der Demo teilnehmen, und ich beschloss mitzugehen. Hungersnot in Afrika ist eine Schande in der heutigen Welt, und es ist wichtig, dass die jüngere Generation ihre Gefühle zeigt: es kann so nicht weitergehen—wir müssen etwas dagegen tun.

Ich habe ein paar andere Jugendliche aus der Schweiz getroffen, und ich war sehr froh und sehr stolz, dass andere Schweizer auch protestieren wollten.

Es war ein einmaliger Tag, denn die Stimmung war ganz entspannt. Die musikalische Begleitung war auch prima—ich habe zum ersten Mal eine Dudelsackkapelle gehört.

(*a*) Why was Ursula in Edinburgh at the time of the demonstration? **1**

(*b*) What prompted her to take part in the demonstration? Write **two** things. **2**

(*c*) What made Ursula feel proud? **1**

DO NOT WRITE IN THIS MARGIN

Marks

3. (continued)

(*d*) What made it such a special day? Write **two** things. 2

Am folgenden Mittwoch bekam ich auch eine Karte für das Live-8-Konzert im Murrayfield-Stadion. Die Mutter meiner Gastfamilie wollte mit ihrem Sohn dahingehen, aber sie ist Krankenschwester und musste im letzten Augenblick arbeiten. Da habe ich ihre Karte bekommen.

Die Atmosphäre im Stadion war schon wieder toll. Die einzige Enttäuschung war, dass es fast den ganzen Abend regnete. Trotz des Regens aber war die ganze Veranstaltung ein großer Erfolg—wir haben die Politiker an ihre Verantwortung gemahnt und das war die Hauptsache.

(*e*) How did Ursula get a ticket for the Live 8 concert at Murrayfield? 1

(*f*) What was the one disappointment about the concert? 1

(*g*) What, according to Ursula, did the concert succeed in doing? 1

Total (26)

[*END OF QUESTION PAPER*]

[BLANK PAGE]

C

1300/409

NATIONAL QUALIFICATIONS 2007

FRIDAY, 25 MAY
2.30 PM – 3.00 PM
(APPROX)

GERMAN
STANDARD GRADE
Credit Level
Listening Transcript

This paper must not be seen by any candidate.

The material overleaf is provided for use in an emergency only (eg the recording or equipment proving faulty) or where permission has been given in advance by SQA for the material to be read to candidates with additional support needs. The material must be read exactly as printed.

Transcript—Credit Level

> **Instructions to reader(s):**
>
> For each item, read the English **once**, then read the German **three times**, with an interval of 5 seconds between the readings. On completion of the third reading, pause for the length of time indicated in brackets after each item, to allow the candidates to write their answers.
>
> Where special arrangements have been agreed in advance to allow the reading of the material, those sections marked **(f)** should be read by a female speaker and those marked **(m)** by a male: those sections marked **(t)** should be read by the teacher.

(t) You are spending two weeks with your exchange partner, Claudia, in Germany.

(f) or (m) **Du verbringst zwei Wochen bei deiner Austauschpartnerin, Claudia, in Deutschland.**

(t) Question number one.

Claudia talks about her favourite group, "Blue Day".

How did she first come across the group? Write **two** things.

(f) **Kennst du die Gruppe „Blue Day"? Das ist meine Lieblingsgruppe. Die Musik habe ich zum ersten Mal gehört, als ich mit meiner Freundin Lisa im Urlaub war. Wir waren auf einem Campingplatz und die Leute im Zelt nebenan haben die CD den ganzen Tag gespielt.**

(*40 seconds*)

(t) Question number two.

Claudia tells you about the group's recent tour of Germany.

When were "Blue Day" on tour in Germany?

What facts show that the tour was a great success? Write **two** things.

(f) **„Blue Day" hat in den Weihnachtsferien eine Deutschlandtournee gemacht. Das war ein Riesenerfolg. Die Karten für alle Konzerte waren innerhalb von zwei Tagen ausverkauft, und bei jedem Konzert waren jeweils über zweitausend Zuschauer. Stell dir das mal vor!**

(*40 seconds*)

(t) Question number three.

Claudia tells you about the concert she and Lisa went to in Frankfurt.

Why was Claudia's mother unable to take them to the concert? How did they get there?

(f) **Lisa und ich haben das Konzert in Frankfurt gesehen. Meine Mutter wollte uns mit dem Auto hinfahren, aber meine Schwester hat sich das Bein gebrochen und Mutti musste sie ins Krankenhaus bringen. Ausgerechnet an diesem Tag! Wir mussten dann mit dem Zug hinfahren.**

(*40 seconds*)

(t) Question number four.

Claudia tells you about music in her school.

What facts show that music is a popular and successful subject in her school? Write **three** things.

(f) **Musik ist ein sehr beliebtes Fach in meiner Schule. Zehn Schüler aus meiner Klasse lernen ein Instrument. Im Schulorchester spielen rund achtzig Jungen und Mädchen. Das ist viel mehr als in anderen Schulen. Und der Schulchor hat dieses Jahr den ersten Preis in einem nationalen Wettbewerb gewonnen.**

(*40 seconds*)

(t) Question number five.

Claudia's dad drives a tour bus round Frankfurt.

Why are there so few tourists on his bus this summer? Write **two** things.

(m) **Ich habe diesen Sommer bisher kaum Touristen in meinem Bus gehabt. Erstens ist es einfach zu heiß, und die Leute haben keine Lust, zwei Stunden in einem Bus zu sitzen. Zweitens ist alles hier in Deutschland so teuer geworden—Busrundfahrten auch.**

(*40 seconds*)

(t) Question number six.

Claudia's dad enjoys his work.

Why does he enjoy it? Write **three** things.

(m) **Meine Arbeit gefällt mir sehr. Es macht Spaß, so viel über die Geschichte der Stadt Frankfurt zu lernen. Ich habe jeden Tag die Gelegenheit, Touristen aus aller Welt zu treffen, und ich habe schon ein paar berühmte Sportler und Musiker in meinem Bus gehabt.**

(*40 seconds*)

(t) Question number seven.

Claudia's dad tells you about the first bus tour he did to Scotland.

When was he first in Scotland?

What did he find difficult? Write **two** things.

(m) **Ich war 1995 zum ersten Mal in Schottland. Es ist ein sehr schönes Land, aber es gab auch ein paar Schwierigkeiten. In Großbritannien fährt man auf der linken Straßenseite und das war ein bisschen komisch. Die Leute hatten auch einen ziemlich starken Akzent, was manchmal problematisch war.**

(*40 seconds*)

[Turn over for Questions 8 to 10 on *Page four*

(t) Question number eight.

Claudia has planned a weekend trip to the town of Rüdesheim.

What kind of accommodation has she booked?

Where is the accommodation? Write **two** things.

(f) **Wir werden das Wochenende in Rüdesheim verbringen. Ich habe Zimmer für uns in einer kleinen Pension gebucht. Sie ist ziemlich zentral gelegen, nur fünf Minuten von dem Fluss entfernt. Es gibt auch viele schöne Weinstuben in der Nähe.**

(40 seconds)

(t) Question number nine.

Claudia's dad talks about the traffic problems in Rüdesheim.

What are the problems? Write **two** things.

(m) **Die Leute in Rüdesheim protestieren im Moment. Es kommen im Sommer zu viele Reisebusse voller Touristen, und die Straßen in Rüdesheim sind viel zu eng dafür. Es kann auch für Kinder und ältere Leute recht gefährlich werden.**

(40 seconds)

(t) Question number ten.

Claudia's dad has his own views on these problems.

What does he say about the problems? Write **two** things.

(m) **Schon gut. Aber Rüdesheim braucht die Touristen und das Geld, das diese mitbringen. Wenn die Stadt im Sommer voller Touristen ist, sind die Geschäfte und Restaurants auch voll.**

(40 seconds)

(t) End of test.

Now look over your answers.

[*END OF TRANSCRIPT*]

FOR OFFICIAL USE

C

Total Mark

1300/408

NATIONAL QUALIFICATIONS 2007

FRIDAY, 25 MAY
2.30 PM – 3.00 PM (APPROX)

GERMAN
STANDARD GRADE
Credit Level
Listening

Fill in these boxes and read what is printed below.

Full name of centre

Town

Forename(s)

Surname

Date of birth
Day Month Year

Scottish candidate number

Number of seat

When you are told to do so, open your paper.

You will hear a number of short items in German. You will hear each item three times, then you will have time to write your answer.

Write your answers, **in English**, in this book, in the appropriate spaces.

You may take notes as you are listening to the German, but only in this paper.

You may **not** use a German dictionary.

You are not allowed to leave the examination room until the end of the test.

Before leaving the examination room you must give this book to the invigilator. If you do not, you may lose all the marks for this paper.

SA 1300/408 6/8970

DO NOT WRITE IN THIS MARGIN

Marks

You are spending two weeks with your exchange partner, Claudia, in Germany.

Du verbringst zwei Wochen bei deiner Austauschpartnerin, Claudia, in Deutschland.

1. Claudia talks about her favourite group, "Blue Day".

How did she first come across the group? Write **two** things. **2**

* * * * *

2. Claudia tells you about the group's recent tour of Germany.

(*a*) When were "Blue Day" on tour in Germany? **1**

(*b*) What facts show that the tour was a great success? Write **two** things. **2**

* * * * *

3. Claudia tells you about the concert she and Lisa went to in Frankfurt.

(*a*) Why was Claudia's mother unable to take them to the concert? **1**

(*b*) How did they get there? **1**

* * * * *

DO NOT WRITE IN THIS MARGIN

Marks

4. Claudia tells you about music in her school.

What facts show that music is a popular and successful subject in her school? Write **three** things. **3**

* * * * *

5. Claudia's dad drives a tour bus round Frankfurt.

Why are there so few tourists on his bus this summer? Write **two** things. **2**

* * * * *

6. Claudia's dad enjoys his work.

Why does he enjoy it? Write **three** things. **3**

* * * * *

[Turn over for Questions 7 to 10 on *Page four*

DO NOT WRITE IN THIS MARGIN

Marks

7. Claudia's dad tells you about the first bus tour he did to Scotland.

(*a*) When was he first in Scotland? **1**

(*b*) What did he find difficult? Write **two** things. **2**

* * * * *

8. Claudia has planned a weekend trip to the town of Rüdesheim.

(*a*) What kind of accommodation has she booked? **1**

(*b*) Where is the accommodation? Write **two** things. **2**

* * * * *

9. Claudia's dad talks about the traffic problems in Rüdesheim.

What are the problems? Write **two** things. **2**

* * * * *

10. Claudia's dad has his own views on these problems.

What does he say about the problems? Write **two** things. **2**

* * * * *

Total (25)

[*END OF QUESTION PAPER*]

STANDARD GRADE | GENERAL

2008

[BLANK PAGE]

FOR OFFICIAL USE

G

Total

1300/402

NATIONAL QUALIFICATIONS 2008

MONDAY, 19 MAY
10.05 AM – 10.50 AM

GERMAN STANDARD GRADE
General Level
Reading

Fill in these boxes and read what is printed below.

Full name of centre

Town

Forename(s)

Surname

Date of birth
Day Month Year

Scottish candidate number

Number of seat

When you are told to do so, open your paper and write your answers **in English** in the spaces provided.

You may use a German dictionary.

Before leaving the examination room you must give this book to the invigilator. If you do not, you may lose all the marks for this paper.

DO NOT WRITE IN THIS MARGIN

Marks

You are reading a German magazine.

1. This survey shows the reasons why people skip breakfast.

Frühstücksumfrage

Warum isst du kein Frühstück?

Es nimmt zu viel Zeit in Anspruch 37%
Morgens habe ich keine Lust auf's Essen.....................28%
Ich bin einfach zu faul...24%
Ich habe Übergewicht und möchte abnehmen.............11%

Why do people skip breakfast? Write the correct percentages in the grid below. **3**

	%
They are on a diet.	
They don't feel like eating.	
It takes too much time.	
They are too lazy.	

Marks DO NOT WRITE IN THIS MARGIN

2. In this article, young people write about their experiences of the 2006 World Cup tournament in Germany.

Was ich am besten fand war die Gastfreundlichkeit der Deutschen.

Luis (Argentinien)

Alle Städte waren so schön und so sauber. Das hat einen guten Eindruck gemacht.

Natacha (Frankreich)

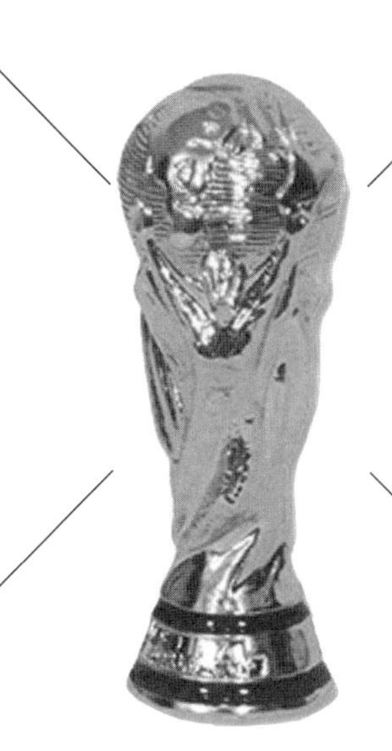

Ich habe sehr viele nette Leute aus der ganzen Welt kennen gelernt.

Pietro (Italien)

Wir hatten auch Zeit, etwas von der Geschichte und den Traditionen des Landes zu lernen.

Kai (Schweden)

Write the correct name in the grid below. **3**

Who . . .

	Name
. . . enjoyed the German hospitality?	
. . . liked learning about German history?	
. . . enjoyed meeting other people?	
. . . was impressed by the cleanliness?	

[Turn over

DO NOT WRITE IN THIS MARGIN

Marks

3. This article is about the smoking ban in Scotland.

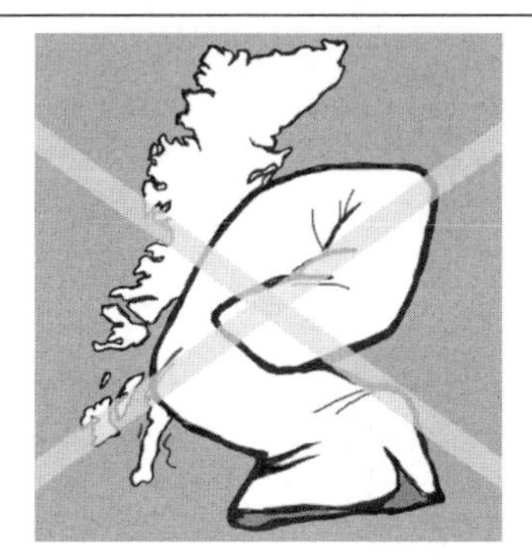

In ganz Schottland herrscht jetzt ein absolutes Rauchverbot in allen Pubs, Restaurants und anderen öffentlich zugänglichen Räumen. Hier einige interessante Fakten:

Wer sich dennoch eine Zigarette anzündet, dem droht eine Geldstrafe von 50 Pfund.

13 000 Schotten sterben jedes Jahr durch das Rauchen.

Durch dieses Verbot hofft man, jährlich 5000 Leben zu retten.

Kritiker fürchten den Verlust von 2500 Arbeitsplätzen.

Why are these numbers mentioned? Fill in the grid below. **4**

Number	**Why is it mentioned?**
50	
13 000	
5000	
2500	

DO NOT WRITE IN THIS MARGIN

Marks

4. In this article, people talk about things that went wrong on their holidays.

Wir waren auf Urlaub in der englischen Universitätsstadt Oxford, und eines Abends brach ein Brand im Hotel aus. Meine Frau hat die Flammen gesehen und sie hat die Feuerwehr rechtzeitig alarmiert.

Thomas

Letzten Sommer war ich in Paris, und jemand hat meinen Koffer am Bahnhof gestohlen. Zum Glück war ich gut versichert, und die Reiseversicherung hat alles schnell gezahlt.

Louisa

Als ich auf Ibiza war, habe ich ein Mofa gemietet. Gleich am ersten Tag hatte ich einen Unfall und brach mir das Bein. Eine nette Familie half mir und brachte mich zu einem Arzt.

Sandra

What went wrong and how was the problem solved? Fill in the grid below. **6**

Name	What went wrong?	How was it solved?
Thomas		
Louisa		
Sandra		

DO NOT WRITE IN THIS MARGIN

Marks

5. You read an interview with Don Kerse, who has recently taken over his own bar.

Seit wann haben Sie die Kneipe hier?
Erst seit sechs Monaten.

Warum haben Sie die Kneipe gekauft?
Der Besitzer wollte die Kneipe verkaufen, denn er wollte wieder nach Hamburg ziehen. Ich arbeite hier seit 10 Jahren, ich kenne alle Gäste gut, ich wohne in der Nachbarschaft, und es war für mich eine gute Chance, endlich mein eigener Boss zu sein.

Haben Sie Pläne für die Kneipe?
Ja, große Pläne. Meine Frau möchte bald warmes Essen servieren, und im Sommer hoffen wir, einen Biergarten hinter der Kneipe zu haben.

Herr Kerse, wir wünschen Ihnen viel Glück mit Ihrer neuen Kneipe.

(*a*) Why did the previous owner decide to sell the bar? **1**

___

(*b*) Why did Don decide to buy the bar? Write **two** things. **2**

___

___

___

(*c*) What plans do Don and his wife have for the bar? Write **two** things. **2**

___

___

___

DO NOT WRITE IN THIS MARGIN

Marks

6. These German teenagers talk about their MP3 players.

Vor vier Wochen habe ich mir einen MP3 Player gekauft. Es gibt farbliche Unterschiede, und ich habe mich für die blaue Variante entschieden. Die gefällt mir am besten.
Stefanie (14)

Die Befestigungsklammer ist eine sehr gute Sache—damit kann man diesen Player auch beim Joggen mitnehmen. Einfach an die Hose klemmen und los geht's.
Ashraf (13)

Alles in allem finde ich den MP3 Player sehr nützlich. Er ist wirklich sehr praktisch, auch wenn er recht teuer ist.
Lukas (15)

Die Menüs hier sind sehr übersichtlich und leicht verständlich. Ich musste mich daran gewöhnen, aber nach ein paar Tagen war das gar kein Problem mehr.
Lena (16)

Write the correct name in the grid below. **3**

Who . . .

	Name
. . . finds it expensive but useful?	
. . . chose it because of the colour?	
. . . likes fastening it to their clothes?	
. . . finds it easy to use?	

[Turn over

Marks

7. These German pupils write about their achievements and interests.

A	**Ich habe den ersten Preis in einem Wettbewerb gewonnen. Ich habe ein Gericht mit Meeresfrüchten gekocht.**
B	**Ich habe schon ein paar Hauptrollen in der Schule gespielt. Ich möchte auf die Schauspielschule gehen.**
C	**In dieser Saison habe ich 20 Tore für meine Schulmannschaft geschossen.**
D	**Ich habe schon meinem Onkel in seiner Werkstatt geholfen und ich kann einen Reifen wechseln.**
E	**Ich zeichne gern und interessiere mich für allerlei Gebäude.**

Match each pupil with a suitable future job. Write the correct letter in each box. **4**

DO NOT WRITE IN THIS MARGIN

Marks

8. This article gives tips on attracting birds to your garden.

- ➢ Pflanzen Sie eine Hecke—das bietet Schutz vor Wind und Wetter
- ➢ Eine Tränke ist sehr wichtig—alle Vögel brauchen frisches Wasser
- ➢ Bei Schnee und Eis regelmäßig füttern
- ➢ Den Futterplatz muss man oft reinigen
- ➢ Vermeiden Sie salzige Nahrung

(*a*) Which tips are mentioned? Tick (✓) **three** boxes. **3**

	Tick (✓)
Keep the garden tidy.	
Plant a hedge.	
Build a bird table.	
Keep the feeding area clean.	
Don't put salty food out.	
Provide a variety of food.	

There is a final reminder for gardeners.

Vögel sind äußerst wichtig im Garten, weil sie sich und ihre Jungen von Raupen und Schnecken ernähren.

(*b*) Why is it important to have birds in your garden? **1**

____

____

Total (32)

[*END OF QUESTION PAPER*]

[BLANK PAGE]

G

1300/407

NATIONAL QUALIFICATIONS 2008

MONDAY, 19 MAY
1.45 PM – 2.10 PM (APPROX)

GERMAN
STANDARD GRADE
General Level
Listening Transcript

This paper must not be seen by any candidate.

The material overleaf is provided for use in an emergency only (eg the recording or equipment proving faulty) or where permission has been given in advance by SQA for the material to be read to candidates with additional support needs. The material must be read exactly as printed.

Transcript—General Level

Instructions to reader(s):

For each item, read the English **once,** then read the German **three times**, with an interval of 5 seconds between the readings. On completion of the third reading, pause for the length of time indicated in brackets after each item, to allow the candidates to write their answers.

Where special arrangements have been agreed in advance to allow the reading of the material, those sections marked **(f)** should be read by a female speaker and those marked **(m)** by a male: those sections marked **(t)** should be read by the teacher.

(t) You are spending a week with your pen friend in Frankfurt. You meet her friends, Steffi and Max.

(f) or (m) **Du verbringst eine Woche bei deiner Brieffreundin in Frankfurt. Du triffst ihre Freunde, Steffi und Max.**

(t) Question number one.

Steffi welcomes you to Frankfurt.

Why does she think you will like the city?

(f) **Willkommen in Frankfurt. Die Stadt wird dir sehr gefallen. Hier gibt es viel für Touristen zu sehen.**

(30 seconds)

(t) Question number two.

Steffi asks you some questions.

What does she ask you? Tick **three** boxes.

(f) **Seit wann lernst du Deutsch? Was machst du in deiner Freizeit? Was für Musik hörst du gern?**

(30 seconds)

(t) Question number three.

Max tells you that he visited Scotland.

What does he tell you? Complete the sentences.

(m) **Ich bin letztes Jahr mit einer Schulgruppe nach Schottland gefahren. Wir haben zehn Tage in einer Jugendherberge verbracht.**

(30 seconds)

(t) Question number four.

Max tells you what he did during his visit.

What did he do? Tick **three** boxes.

(m) **In Schottland habe ich so viel gemacht und gesehen. Wir haben schöne Wanderungen in den Bergen gemacht, wir haben mehrere interessante Schlösser besucht, und am letzten Tag haben wir ein paar Stunden in einer Reitschule verbracht.**

(30 seconds)

(t) **Question number five.**

Max tells you how he travelled to Scotland.

How did he travel? Tick the correct box.

(m) **Wir sind mit der Fähre von Belgien direkt nach Schottland gefahren. Das war sehr praktisch.**

(30 seconds)

(t) **Question number six.**

Max tells you that they wanted to fly.

Why was this not possible? Write **two** things.

(m) **Wir wollten eigentlich nach Schottland fliegen, aber die Flugpreise waren einfach zu hoch. Außerdem hatten wir zu viel Gepäck.**

(30 seconds)

(t) **Question number seven.**

Max tells you that he noticed a difference between Scotland and Germany.

What was the difference?

(m) **In Schottland waren die meisten Geschäfte auch am Sonntag offen. Das sieht man in Deutschland fast nie.**

(30 seconds)

(t) **Question number eight.**

Max tried fish and chips in Scotland.

What does he say about it? Write **two** things.

(m) **Fisch mit Pommes—das hat mir geschmeckt. Aber mit so viel Fett ist es nicht gesund. Das sollte man nicht jeden Tag essen.**

(30 seconds)

(t) **Question number nine.**

Steffi suggests you go to the cinema tonight.

What kind of film is showing? Tick the correct box.

When did her brother see the film? Complete the sentence.

(f) **Habt ihr Lust, heute Abend ins Kino zu gehen? Es läuft ein toller Liebesfilm. Mein Bruder hat ihn vor drei Tagen gesehen und fand ihn echt gut.**

(30 seconds)

[Turn over for Questions 10, 11, 12 and 13 on *Page four*

(t) **Question number ten.**

Max doesn't want to go to the cinema.

Why does he not want to go? Write **two** things.

(m) **Es tut mir leid. Ich will nicht mitkommen. Gestern Nacht habe ich nicht gut geschlafen und jetzt habe ich Kopfschmerzen.**

(30 seconds)

(t) **Question number eleven.**

Steffi decides to stay at home instead.

What does she suggest you do? Write **two** things.

(f) **Bleiben wir also lieber zu Hause. Wir könnten auf der Terrasse im Garten sitzen und die Pläne für nächste Woche besprechen. Was meint ihr?**

(30 seconds)

(t) **Question number twelve.**

You talk about school.

What does Steffi say about her teachers? Write **two** things.

(f) **Jetzt gefällt mir die Schule ganz gut. Die meisten Lehrer sind ziemlich streng, aber sie behandeln uns nicht mehr wie kleine Kinder.**

(30 seconds)

(t) **Question number thirteen.**

Steffi talks about going abroad to work when she leaves school.

Why does she want to go abroad? Tick **two** boxes.

Who will help her to find a job abroad?

(f) **Nach der Schule möchte ich ein paar Jahre im Ausland verbringen. Ich möchte meine Sprachkenntnisse verbessern und ich will auch Arbeitserfahrung sammeln. Ein Kollege meines Vaters wird mir helfen, eine Stelle zu finden.**

(30 seconds)

(t) **End of test.**

Now look over your answers.

[*END OF TRANSCRIPT*]

FOR OFFICIAL USE

G

Total Mark

1300/406

NATIONAL QUALIFICATIONS 2008

MONDAY, 19 MAY
1.45 PM – 2.10 PM (APPROX)

GERMAN
STANDARD GRADE
General Level
Listening

Fill in these boxes and read what is printed below.

Full name of centre

Town

Forename(s)

Surname

Date of birth
Day Month Year

Scottish candidate number

Number of seat

When you are told to do so, open your paper.

You will hear a number of short items in German. You will hear each item three times, then you will have time to write your answer.

Write your answers, **in English**, in this book, in the appropriate spaces.

You may take notes as you are listening to the German, but only in this book.

You may **not** use a German dictionary.

You are not allowed to leave the examination room until the end of the test.

Before leaving the examination room you must give this book to the invigilator. If you do not, you may lose all the marks for this paper.

SA 1300/406 6/12070

DO NOT WRITE IN THIS MARGIN

Marks

You are spending a week with your pen friend in Frankfurt. You meet her friends, Steffi and Max.

Du verbringst eine Woche bei deiner Brieffreundin in Frankfurt. Du triffst ihre Freunde, Steffi und Max.

1. Steffi welcomes you to Frankfurt.

Why does she think you will like the city?

____ **1**

* * * * *

2. Steffi asks you some questions.

What does she ask you? Tick (✓) **three** boxes. **3**

	Tick (✓)
How long have you been learning German?	
Do you like learning German?	
Do you have a lot of spare time?	
What do you do in your spare time?	
Do you like listening to music?	
What kind of music do you like?	

* * * * *

3. Max tells you that he visited Scotland.

What does he tell you? Complete the sentences. **2**

He went with ______________________________ .

They stayed in a ______________________________ .

* * * * *

DO NOT WRITE IN THIS MARGIN

Marks

4. Max tells you what he did during his visit.

What did he do? Tick (✓) **three** boxes. **3**

* * * * *

5. Max tells you how he travelled to Scotland.

How did he travel? Tick (✓) the correct box. **1**

* * * * *

6. Max tells you that they wanted to fly.

Why was this not possible? Write **two** things. **2**

____

____

____

* * * * *

Marks

7. Max tells you that he noticed a difference between Scotland and Germany.

What was the difference? **1**

____

____

* * * * *

8. Max tried fish and chips in Scotland.

What does he say about it? Write **two** things. **2**

____

____

____

* * * * *

9. Steffi suggests you go to the cinema tonight.

(*a*) What kind of film is showing? Tick (✓) the correct box. **1**

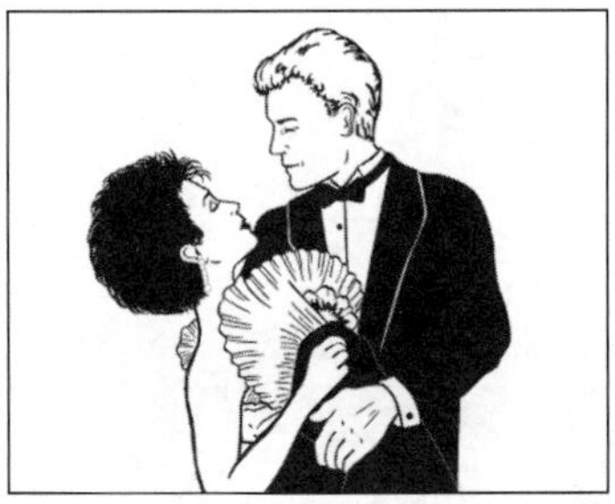

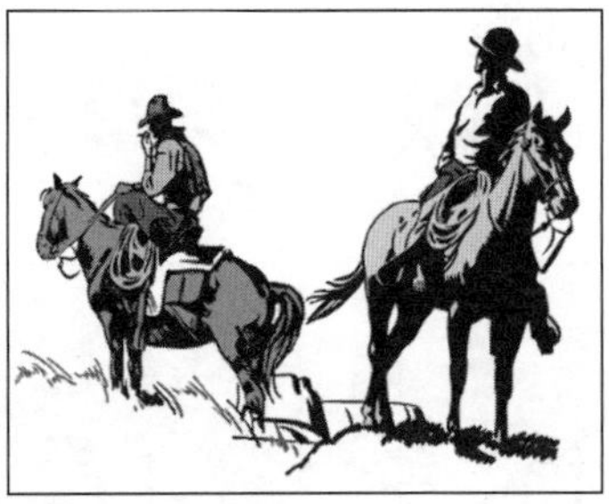

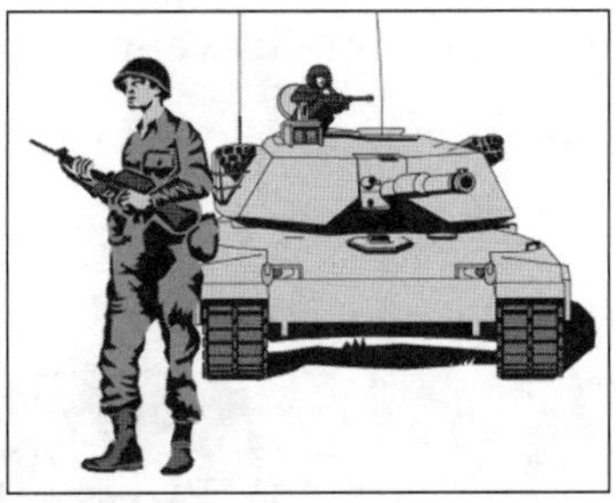

☐ ☐ ☐

(*b*) When did her brother see the film? Complete the sentence. **1**

He saw the film ______________________________.

* * * * *

10. Max doesn't want to go to the cinema.

Why does he not want to go? Write **two** things. **2**

____

____

* * * * *

DO NOT WRITE IN THIS MARGIN

Marks

11. Steffi decides to stay at home instead.

What does she suggest you do? Write **two** things. **2**

* * * * *

12. You talk about school.

What does Steffi say about her teachers? Write **two** things. **2**

* * * * *

13. Steffi talks about going abroad to work when she leaves school.

(*a*) Why does she want to go abroad? Tick (✓) **two** boxes. **2**

	Tick (✓)
To meet new people	
To improve her language skills	
To be more independent	
To gain work experience	
To earn money	

(*b*) Who will help her to find a job abroad? **1**

* * * * *

Total (26)

[*END OF QUESTION PAPER*]

[BLANK PAGE]

STANDARD GRADE | CREDIT

2008

[BLANK PAGE]

FOR OFFICIAL USE

C

Total

1300/403

NATIONAL QUALIFICATIONS 2008

MONDAY, 19 MAY
11.10 AM – 12.10 PM

GERMAN
STANDARD GRADE
Credit Level
Reading

Fill in these boxes and read what is printed below.

Full name of centre

Town

Forename(s)

Surname

Date of birth
Day Month Year

Scottish candidate number

Number of seat

When you are told to do so, open your paper and write your answers **in English** in the spaces provided.

You may use a German dictionary.

Before leaving the examination room you must give this book to the invigilator. If you do not, you may lose all the marks for this paper.

Marks

You are reading a German magazine.

1. This article is about a girl called Heidi, who started her own theatre group.

Ich wollte schon immer Schauspielerin werden, und als ich zehn Jahre alt war, schlug meine Mutter eines Tages vor, dass ich zu einer Theatergruppe gehen sollte. Das war aber nicht so einfach: Viele Theatergruppen der Stadt waren für Jugendliche im Alter von dreizehn oder vierzehn Jahren bestimmt, und die anderen waren zu weit weg am Stadtrand.

(*a*) Why did Heidi find it difficult to join a theatre group? Write **two** things. **2**

____

____

____

Ich habe also meine eigene Theatergruppe gegründet. Mit Hilfe meiner Eltern habe ich ein Inserat in der Regionalzeitung aufgegeben. In der ersten Woche haben sich mehr als dreißig Kinder bei uns gemeldet, und ich muss sagen, dass ich regelrecht erstaunt war. Dann habe ich mir aber ein paar wichtige Fragen gestellt: Wo finden wir einen Regisseur für das Theaterstück? Werden wir die Aula in der Schule mieten können?

(*b*) How did Heidi go about getting people to join her group? **1**

____

____

DO NOT WRITE IN THIS MARGIN

Marks

1. (continued)

(*c*) Exactly how successful were her efforts to get people to join? **1**

(*d*) Once people had joined, what did Heidi have to consider? Write **two** things. **2**

Die erste Vorstellung fand kurz vor Weihnachten statt. Sie war leider eine reine Katastrophe, und wir waren alle so enttäuscht. Wir hatten nur zwei kleine Scheinwerfer, und gleich am ersten Abend gingen sie kaputt. Am zweiten Abend hatte der Hauptdarsteller eine furchtbare Mandelentzündung, und er war so heiser, dass man ihn kaum hören konnte.

(*e*) The group put on a show before Christmas.

What went wrong? Complete the sentences. **2**

On the first evening ______________________________

____

______________________________.

On the second evening ______________________________

____

______________________________.

[Turn over

Marks

2. This article is about teenage problems.

Für Jugendliche heute gibt es allerlei Probleme, und die jungen Leute müssen lernen, diese Probleme selber zu lösen. Jugendliche müssen Freunde haben oder zu einer Clique gehören, wenn sie ein gesundes Selbstbewusstsein aufbauen wollen. Ein häufiges Problem aber ist Gruppenzwang*. Wenn die Gruppe eine bestimmte Mode vorzieht, muss man auch unbedingt diese Kleider kaufen, oder wenn die Freunde ihre Hausaufgaben vernachlässigen, macht man das auch. Viele Teenager können diesem Druck nicht widerstehen.

* Gruppenzwang = peer pressure

(*a*) Why is it important for teenagers to have friends? **1**

____

____

(*b*) What do teenagers do because of peer pressure? Write **two** things. **2**

____

____

____

DO NOT WRITE IN THIS MARGIN

Marks

2. (continued)

Jugendliche drücken ihre Probleme ganz unterschiedlich aus. Manche haben Krach mit den Eltern. Andere verkriechen sich in ihrem Zimmer und verbringen viel Zeit allein. Als Eltern sollten Sie in erster Linie Freunde sein und weniger Eltern. Besprechen Sie alles mit Ihren Teenagern, nehmen Sie sie und ihre Probleme ernst, behandeln Sie sie wie erwachsene Menschen.

(*c*) Teenagers react differently to problems. In what **two** completely **different** ways do they react? **2**

(*d*) What should parents do to help teenagers? Write any **three** things. **3**

Jugendliche wollen ihre Geheimnisse haben und gehen nicht mehr mit jedem Problem zu ihren Eltern. Gudrun Junker (16), aus Hamburg, ist ein gutes Beispiel dafür: „Meine Mutter ist manchmal sauer auf mich, zum Beispiel, wenn ich mein ganzes Taschengeld an einem Tag ausgebe. Ich kann mit ihr nicht über meine Probleme reden. Es liegt vielleicht auch an mir, warum ich mich nicht mit meinen Eltern verstehe— ich bin ja fast nie zu Hause.“

(*e*) When does Gudrun's mother get annoyed with her? **1**

(*f*) Gudrun feels that the problems with her parents are perhaps her fault.

Why is this? **1**

Marks

3. This article is about ideal jobs.

Ein deutsches Forschungsinstitut hat neulich über zweitausend Arbeitnehmer in vielen verschiedenen Arbeitsbereichen gefragt: „Wie sehen Sie Ihren Traumjob?“ Die Ergebnisse waren sehr interessant. Fast alle Arbeitnehmer wollten viel mehr Abwechslung, und sie schätzten vor allem den häufigen Kontakt zu anderen Menschen. Die größte Überraschung war, dass ein hohes Gehalt für viele Menschen keine große Rolle spielt.

(*a*) What did a recent job survey reveal as being important to most employees? Write **two** things. **2**

____

____

____

(*b*) What was the most surprising fact to come out of the survey? **1**

____

____

DO NOT WRITE IN THIS MARGIN

Marks

3. (continued)

Viele Menschen spüren, dass sie mit ihrem Job unzufrieden sind, aber sie haben noch nicht über mögliche Alternativen nachgedacht. Ihr erstes Ziel sollte also sein, eine Beschreibung für einen idealen Job zu formulieren. Diese Aufgabe ist ganz einfach. Am besten sollte man das in einer ruhigen Stunde machen. Man sollte nicht zu lange überlegen, sondern die neuen Einfälle schnell und spontan hinschreiben.

(*c*) What is the first thing people should do when considering a new job? **1**

(*d*) What is the best way of doing this? Write **two** things. **2**

Es ist auch sinnvoll, an den allerschlimmsten Job zu denken. Man kann sich folgende Fragen stellen: Was sind für Sie die schlimmsten Arbeitsbedingungen, die Sie sich vorstellen können? Mit welchen Kollegen könnten Sie unter keinen Umständen arbeiten? Wenn man diese zwei Fragen beantwortet hat, wird es hoffentlich viel einfacher sein, den ersehnten Traumjob zu finden.

(*e*) The article says that you should imagine the worst possible job.

What points should you consider when thinking of this job? Write **two** things. **2**

Total (26)

[*END OF QUESTION PAPER*]

[BLANK PAGE]

C

1300/409

NATIONAL QUALIFICATIONS 2008

MONDAY, 19 MAY
2.30 PM – 3.00 PM
(APPROX)

GERMAN
STANDARD GRADE
Credit Level
Listening Transcript

This paper must not be seen by any candidate.

The material overleaf is provided for use in an emergency only (eg the recording or equipment proving faulty) or where permission has been given in advance by SQA for the material to be read to candidates with additional support needs. The material must be read exactly as printed.

SA 1300/409 6/680

Transcript—Credit Level

Instructions to reader(s):

For each item, read the English **once**, then read the German **three times**, with an interval of 5 seconds between the readings. On completion of the third reading, pause for the length of time indicated in brackets after each item, to allow the candidates to write their answers.

Where special arrangements have been agreed in advance to allow the reading of the material, those sections marked **(f)** should be read by a female speaker and those marked **(m)** by a male: those sections marked **(t)** should be read by the teacher.

(t) You are staying with your pen friend, Gabi, in Austria.

(f) or (m) **Du wohnst bei deiner Brieffreundin, Gabi, in Österreich.**

(t) Question number one.

Gabi tells you about her part-time job in a café.

What is the good thing about her job?

Why does she not get on with her boss? Write **two** things.

(f) **Seit einem Jahr arbeite ich als Kellnerin in einem Café. Ich verdiene zwar ziemlich gut, aber mit meiner Chefin komme ich nicht gut aus. Sie streitet mit den Kunden und ist oft sehr unhöflich. Sie hat auch keine neuen Ideen für das Café, und das ist schade.**

(*40 seconds*)

(t) Question number two.

Gabi would like to make some changes to the café.

What changes would she like to make? Write **three** things.

(f) **Das Café ist zu dunkel. Man sollte weiße oder helle Vorhänge haben. Für die Gäste sollte man eine bessere Auswahl an Zeitschriften und Zeitungen haben. Ich würde auch ein paar Gerichte aus Italien oder Frankreich einführen, um die Speisekarte interessanter zu machen.**

(*40 seconds*)

(t) Question number three.

Gabi wants to continue working in the café.

Why is this? Write **two** things.

(f) **Ich werde voraussichtlich im Café weiterarbeiten. Ich muss mein Studium finanzieren und ich mache mir viele Sorgen deswegen. Mein Vater ist im Moment arbeitslos und kann mir deshalb keine finanzielle Unterstützung bieten.**

(*40 seconds*)

(t) Question number four.

You talk about leisure time.

According to Gabi, why is it important to have leisure time? Write **two** things.

(f) **Im Moment habe ich nicht viel Freizeit, weil ich so viel arbeiten muss. Freizeit ist aber wichtig, weil man Zeit für sich selbst braucht. Man muss auch die Gelegenheit haben, Freunde außerhalb der Schule zu treffen.**

(*40 seconds*)

(t) Question number five.

Gabi's brother, Alex, talks about his new school building.

What does he say is wrong with it? Write **two** things.

(m) **Im neuen Schulgebäude, das man erst letztes Jahr gebaut hat, gibt es nicht genug Platz für alle Schüler, und die Klassenzimmer sind einfach zu eng. Die neuen Fahrradständer sind am anderen Ende des Schulhofs und nicht mehr direkt am Eingang.**

(*40 seconds*)

(t) Question number six.

Alex thinks that the old school building was better.

Why does he think this? Write **two** things.

(m) **Das alte Gebäude war weitaus besser als das neue. Es war ein historisches Gebäude aus roten Backsteinen und sah viel schöner aus. Im Sommer waren die Klassenzimmer schön kühl. Ja, ich vermisse das alte Gebäude sehr.**

(*40 seconds*)

(t) Question number seven.

Gabi wants to go to an art exhibition in town today.

Why does she want to go to the exhibition? Write **two** things.

What exactly does she say about the artist?

(f) **Im Moment gibt es eine Ausstellung in der Staatsgalerie. Für alle Schüler und Studenten ist der Eintritt kostenlos. Letztes Jahr habe ich einen interessanten Artikel über diesen Maler gelesen und ich muss diese Ausstellung unbedingt sehen. Der Maler ist 1975 aus Russland nach Österreich gekommen.**

(*40 seconds*)

[Turn over for Questions 8 to 10 on *Page four*

(t) Question number eight.

Alex cannot go to the exhibition today.

Why can't he go? Write **two** things.

(m) **Ich möchte schon in die Galerie mitkommen, ich kann aber nicht. Ich habe meinem Freund versprochen, mit ihm Getränke für seine Party vom Supermarkt zu holen. Dann müssen wir am frühen Abend Freunde am Bahnhof abholen.**

(*40 seconds*)

(t) Question number nine.

Before you go out, Gabi offers to make her own soup for lunch.

Why does she want to make her own soup? Write **three** things.

(f) **Wie wär's, wenn ich etwas zum Mittagessen mache? Ich werde eine Gemüsesuppe kochen. Dosensuppe enthält weniger Vitamine als selbstgemachte Suppe. Frisches Gemüse aus dem eigenen Garten schmeckt immer so gut, und in einer halben Stunde ist die Suppe schon auf dem Tisch.**

(*40 seconds*)

(t) Question number ten.

At lunch, Alex talks about his colleagues' eating habits.

What is unhealthy about their eating habits? Write **three** things.

(m) **Viele meiner Kollegen finden es unmöglich, gesunde Sachen zu essen. Sie arbeiten in der Mittagspause und essen sehr wenig oder gar nichts. Sie sind dann am Abend so müde, dass sie keine Lust haben, etwas Richtiges zu kochen, und sie holen sich lieber etwas vom Schnellimbiss. Das ist gar nicht gesund, finde ich.**

(*40 seconds*)

(t) End of test.

Now look over your answers.

[*END OF TRANSCRIPT*]

FOR OFFICIAL USE

C

Total Mark

1300/408

NATIONAL QUALIFICATIONS 2008

MONDAY, 19 MAY
2.30 PM – 3.00 PM (APPROX)

GERMAN STANDARD GRADE
Credit Level
Listening

Fill in these boxes and read what is printed below.

Full name of centre

Town

Forename(s)

Surname

Date of birth
Day Month Year

Scottish candidate number

Number of seat

When you are told to do so, open your paper.

You will hear a number of short items in German. You will hear each item three times, then you will have time to write your answer.

Write your answers, **in English**, in this book, in the appropriate spaces.

You may take notes as you are listening to the German, but only in this book.

You may **not** use a German dictionary.

You are not allowed to leave the examination room until the end of the test.

Before leaving the examination room you must give this book to the invigilator. If you do not, you may lose all the marks for this paper.

SA 1300/408 6/9870

DO NOT WRITE IN THIS MARGIN

Marks

You are staying with your pen friend, Gabi, in Austria.

Du wohnst bei deiner Brieffreundin, Gabi, in Österreich.

1. Gabi tells you about her part-time job in a café.

(*a*) What is the good thing about her job? **1**

(*b*) Why does she not get on with her boss? Write **two** things. **2**

* * * * *

2. Gabi would like to make some changes to the café.

What changes would she like to make? Write **three** things. **3**

* * * * *

3. Gabi wants to continue working in the café.

Why is this? Write **two** things. **2**

* * * * *

DO NOT WRITE IN THIS MARGIN

Marks

4. You talk about leisure time.

According to Gabi, why is it important to have leisure time? Write **two** things. **2**

* * * * *

5. Gabi's brother, Alex, talks about his new school building.

What does he say is wrong with it? Write **two** things. **2**

* * * * *

6. Alex thinks that the old school building was better.

Why does he think this? Write **two** things. **2**

* * * * *

7. Gabi wants to go to an art exhibition in town today.

(*a*) Why does she want to go to the exhibition? Write **two** things. **2**

(*b*) What exactly does she say about the artist? **1**

* * * * *

[Turn over for Questions 8 to 10 on *Page four*

DO NOT WRITE IN THIS MARGIN

Marks

8. Alex cannot go to the exhibition today.

Why can't he go? Write **two** things. **2**

* * * * *

9. Before you go out, Gabi offers to make her own soup for lunch.

Why does she want to make her own soup? Write **three** things. **3**

* * * * *

10. At lunch, Alex talks about his colleagues' eating habits.

What is unhealthy about their eating habits? Write **three** things. **3**

* * * * *

Total (25)

[*END OF QUESTION PAPER*]

STANDARD GRADE | GENERAL

2009

[BLANK PAGE]

FOR OFFICIAL USE

G

Total

1300/402

NATIONAL QUALIFICATIONS 2009

WEDNESDAY, 20 MAY
10.50 AM – 11.35 AM

GERMAN STANDARD GRADE

General Level Reading

Fill in these boxes and read what is printed below.

Full name of centre

Town

Forename(s)

Surname

Date of birth
Day Month Year

Scottish candidate number

Number of seat

When you are told to do so, open your paper and write your answers **in English** in the spaces provided.

You may use a German dictionary.

Before leaving the examination room you must give this book to the invigilator. If you do not, you may lose all the marks for this paper.

SA 1300/402 6/11520

Marks

You are reading a German magazine.

1. You read an article about a new youth centre.

Neues Jugendzentrum hier in Burgdorf

Im kommenden Sommer werden wir ein neues Jugendzentrum in Burgdorf haben. Gut ist, dass die jungen Leute viel mehr Platz haben werden. Das neue Zentrum wird auch bessere Sportmöglichkeiten haben.

Ein paar Leute sagen aber, dass das neue Zentrum ein hässliches Gebäude ist, mit zu viel Beton.

(*a*) What are the good points of the new youth centre? Write **two** things. **2**

____

____

(*b*) Some people do not like the new centre. Why is this? **1**

____

DO NOT WRITE IN THIS MARGIN

Marks

2. Karl writes about his town.

Ich habe mein ganzes Leben in dieser Stadt gewohnt. Für Jugendliche ist hier viel los. Es gibt aber fast keine guten Geschäfte, und man muss in die nächste Stadt fahren, um einkaufen zu gehen. Da die Stadt ziemlich klein ist, gibt es wenige Probleme mit Verkehr. Es gibt aber viel Abfall auf der Straße. Das finde ich ärgerlich.

Are his comments about the following **positive** or **negative**?

Tick (✓) the correct box for each one. **3**

	Positive	**Negative**
Entertainment for teenagers		
Shops		
Litter		

[Turn over

Marks

3. This article is about a cinema for children.

Kinderkino—eine tolle Idee

Vier- bis achtjährige Kinder haben jetzt ihr eigenes Kino. Jeden Samstag bieten wir ein Filmprogramm für die jüngsten Kinobesucher. Vor dem Film können die Kinder zusammen spielen. Die Filme sind kurz und sind für Kinder geeignet. Wir bieten gleichzeitig Filme für Erwachsene. So haben Eltern die Gelegenheit, ohne Babysitter und ohne Aufpreis einen neuen Film zu sehen.

(*a*) Why is this cinema ideal for children? Write **two** things. **2**

____

____

____

(*b*) Why is it suitable for parents? **1**

____

____

DO NOT WRITE IN THIS MARGIN

Marks

4. This article gives advice on staying safe while on holiday.

Ohne Angst in den Urlaub

- Vergiss nicht, dass ein Unfall zu jeder Zeit geschehen kann, besonders wenn man die Ferien am Meer verbringt.
- Bei starken Magenschmerzen sollte man besser zur Apotheke oder zum Arzt gehen.
- Alle 23 Sekunden werden Urlauber Opfer eines Diebstahls. Seien Sie besonders vorsichtig an Sehenswürdigkeiten, auf Märkten, in öffentlichen Verkehrsmitteln und am Frühstücksbuffet im Hotel.

(*a*) What advice does the article give? Complete the sentences. **2**

- Remember that accidents can happen anywhere, especially ________

____.

- If you have stomach pains you should ________________

____.

(*b*) The article tells you to be wary of thieves in certain places.

Which of the following is **not** mentioned? Tick (✓) the correct box. **1**

	Tick
Tourist attractions	
Airports	
Public transport	

[Turn over

DO NOT WRITE IN THIS MARGIN

Marks

5. You read an interview with Martin Klee, who works on a ferry boat in Germany.

- **Herr Klee, wie finden Sie die Arbeit auf der Fähre?**

Ich arbeite sehr gern auf dem Boot. Die meisten Passagiere sind recht nett und freundlich. Ich muss aber sagen, dass ich mich ärgere, wenn die Leute unhöflich sind.

- **Wird die Arbeit manchmal langweilig?**

Eigentlich nicht. Ich muss verschiedene Sachen auf der Fähre machen. Ich muss dafür sorgen, dass alle Autos sicher auf das Boot kommen. Das ist eine sehr verantwortungsvolle Aufgabe. Ich muss dann prüfen, dass alle Fahrgäste eine gültige Karte haben. Auch muss ich das Boot streichen.

(*a*) When does Martin get annoyed? **1**

____

(*b*) What jobs does he do on the ferry? Write any **two** things. **2**

____

____

____

DO NOT WRITE IN THIS MARGIN

Marks

6. This article is about cycling in the city.

Viele junge Leute fahren sehr gern mit dem Rad. So kann man in der Stadt Staus vermeiden, und durch's Radfahren kann man auch schlank bleiben. Es gibt aber auch Probleme für Radfahrer, besonders in der Großstadt. Autofahrer sind oft rücksichtslos, wenn sie in der Hauptverkehrszeit zur Arbeit fahren. In vielen Städten gibt es Radwege, aber sie sind oft zu eng, und auch das ist gefährlich für Radfahrer.

(*a*) Why is cycling popular with young people? Write **two** things. **2**

____

____

(*b*) When are car drivers often inconsiderate towards cyclists? **1**

____

(*c*) Why are some cycle paths dangerous for cyclists? **1**

____

[Turn over

Marks

7. These young Germans write about a school exchange to Scotland.

Was mir am besten gefallen hat, war meine Gastfamilie. Sie haben alles für mich gemacht und sie waren alle so freundlich und großzügig.

Max

Meine Partnerin und ich sind ziemlich oft wandern gegangen. Ich habe viel gesehen, und die Landschaft war sehr schön. Leider hat es oft geregnet und es war sehr nass.

Anna

Die Essgewohnheiten der Schotten waren mir fremd. Das Frühstück jeden Morgen war sehr fettig und ziemlich ungesund.

Stefan

Die Mutter meiner Gastfamilie hat alles selber gekocht, und ich fand das Essen wirklich lecker. Ich habe sogar ein schottisches Kochbuch für meine Mutter gekauft.

Selassi

Gut war, dass ich mein eigenes Zimmer hatte. Es war groß und sehr modern. Es gab einen Spielraum im Dachgeschoss, wo mein Partner und ich Snooker gespielt haben.

Frank

Write the correct name in each box. **4**

Who liked . . .

	Name
. . . the accommodation?	
. . . the scenery?	
. . . the people they stayed with?	
. . . the food?	

DO NOT WRITE IN THIS MARGIN

Marks

8. Some pupils give advice on how to approach school work.

Man sollte nie nach dem Mittagessen oder nach dem Abendessen lernen.

Vadim

Man sollte immer einen ordentlichen Arbeitsplatz haben, wo alles bereit liegt. So kann man schneller und auch besser lernen.

Karla

Keine Panik! Wenn die Klassenkameraden bessere Noten haben, ist das keine Katastrophe. Du brauchst beim Lernen Ziele, die du erreichen kannst.

Julia

What advice do they give? Write the correct name in each box. **3**

	Name
It doesn't matter if others do better than you.	
Organise your work area.	
Don't study after having a meal.	

[Turn over

Marks

9. These young people write about television.

Ich sehe nie fern, weil ich keine Zeit dazu habe. Vormittags gehe ich in die Schule und nachmittags gehe ich zum Tennistraining. Am Abend bin ich dann zu müde, um fernzusehen.

Nina (14)

Ich kann sehen, was ich will, denn ich habe einen Fernseher in meinem Zimmer. Ich liebe Fernsehen, weil ich mich dabei entspanne. Musiksendungen finde ich toll.

Axel (16)

Ich sehe gern fern, aber mein Vater ist nicht einverstanden. Wir haben eine Abmachung getroffen: Ich darf drei Abende die Woche fernsehen, aber nicht mehr.

Andreas (15)

Are the following statements **True** or **False**? Tick (✓) the correct box for each one. **3**

	True	**False**
Nina likes watching sport on TV.		
Axel finds watching TV relaxing.		
Andreas is allowed to watch TV whenever he wants.		

DO NOT WRITE IN THIS MARGIN

Marks

10. You read an article about the city of Cologne.

Köln ist eine faszinierende Stadt. Im Sommer wird die Stadt zu einem Treffpunkt für Menschen aus aller Welt.

Der Dom hier ist weltbekannt—der Bau begann in dem Jahr 1248 und dauerte über 600 Jahre. Der Dom ist das zweithöchste Gebäude der Stadt—nur der Fernsehturm ist höher.

Köln liegt am Rhein und von einem Schiff auf dem Fluss hat man den besten Blick auf die Stadt.

(*a*) What happens to the city in summer? **1**

____

____

(*b*) What is the tallest building in the city? **1**

____

(*c*) Where is the best place to get a view of the city? **1**

____

Total (32)

[*END OF QUESTION PAPER*]

[BLANK PAGE]

G

1300/407

NATIONAL QUALIFICATIONS 2009

WEDNESDAY, 20 MAY
11.55 AM – 12.20 PM
(APPROX)

GERMAN
STANDARD GRADE
General Level
Listening Transcript

This paper must not be seen by any candidate.

The material overleaf is provided for use in an emergency only (eg the recording or equipment proving faulty) or where permission has been given in advance by SQA for the material to be read to candidates with additional support needs. The material must be read exactly as printed.

SA 1300/407 6/1410

Transcript—General Level

Instructions to reader(s):

For each item, read the English **once**, then read the German **three times**, with an interval of 5 seconds between the readings. On completion of the third reading, pause for the length of time indicated in brackets after each item, to allow the candidates to write their answers.

Where special arrangements have been agreed in advance to allow the reading of the material, those sections marked **(f)** should be read by a female speaker and those marked **(m)** by a male; those sections marked **(t)** should be read by the teacher.

(t) You are on holiday in Majorca. You meet two young Germans, Boris and Jutta.

(f) or (m) **Du bist im Urlaub auf Mallorca. Du triffst zwei junge Deutsche, Boris und Jutta.**

(t) Question number one.

You chat to Boris about their holiday.

Are the statements **True** or **False**? Tick the correct box for each one.

What does Boris ask you?

(m) **Wir finden Mallorca sehr schön und kommen jedes Jahr hierher. Wir sind erst heute angekommen und werden zwei Wochen hier verbringen. Bist du zum ersten Mal hier?**

(*30 seconds*)

(t) Question number two.

Boris talks about how cheap it is to get to Majorca.

What does he say? Complete the sentence.

(m) **Die Reise ist immer so billig. Ein Flug nach Mallorca kostet weniger als eine Zugfahrt in Deutschland.**

(*30 seconds*)

(t) Question number three.

Jutta tells you that her parents also like Majorca.

Why is Majorca special to them?

(f) **Hier auf Mallorca haben sich mein Vater und meine Mutter getroffen. Das war vor zwanzig Jahren. Deshalb lieben sie Mallorca sehr.**

(*30 seconds*)

(t) Question number four.

Jutta tells you there is a beach nearby.

What does she say about it? Write **three** things.

(f) **Es gibt einen Strand hier in der Nähe. Dort ist das Wasser ein klares Blau. Der Strand selbst ist sehr sauber und auch ruhig. Du musst auf jeden Fall da hingehen.**

(*30 seconds*)

(t) Question number five.

Jutta talks about restaurants.

What does she say about the restaurants in town? Tick **two** boxes.

What type of food does she prefer? Complete the sentence.

(f) **In der Altstadt gibt es eine große Auswahl an Restaurants, die ganztags geöffnet sind. Das Essen ist wirklich preiswert. Ich esse am liebsten vegetarisch.**

(*30 seconds*)

(t) Question number six.

Boris talks about his favourite restaurant.

Where exactly is the restaurant? Tick the correct box.

What is the restaurant's speciality? Complete the sentence.

(m) **Ich empfehle das Restaurant *Darsena* am Hafen. Der Blick ist wunderschön. Das *Darsena* hat sich auf Fleischgerichte spezialisiert und bietet über vierzig Gerichte an! Mein Lieblingsgericht ist Schweinekotelett.**

(*30 seconds*)

(t) Question number seven.

Jutta tells you what happened to her during last year's holiday.

What happened? Write **two** things.

(f) **Eines Tages war es dreißig Grad. Ich bin zu lange in der Sonne geblieben. Ich bin eingeschlafen und habe einen Sonnenbrand bekommen.**

(*30 seconds*)

(t) Question number eight.

Boris gives you advice about staying safe in the sun.

What does he say you should do? Write **three** things.

(m) **Im Hochsommer kann die Sonne sehr gefährlich sein. Vor allen Dingen sollte man eine gute Sonnencreme benutzen und einen Sonnenhut tragen. Am besten sollte man auch unter einem Sonnenschirm oder im Schatten bleiben.**

(*30 seconds*)

[Turn over for Questions 9 to 12 on *Page four*

(t) Question number nine.

Jutta tells you she plans to go shopping.

What is she going to buy? Tick the correct box.

What does she say about the department stores? Complete the sentences.

(f) **Morgen fahre ich nach Palma zum Einkaufen. Ich würde gern ein paar Geschenke kaufen. Man kann stundenlang shoppen gehen, da die meisten Kaufhäuser bis spät am Abend geöffnet sind. Ich finde die Verkäufer hilfsbereit.**

(*30 seconds*)

(t) Question number ten.

Boris tells you he doesn't want to go shopping.

Why does he not want to go? Complete the sentence.

(m) **Ich will nicht einkaufen gehen. Ich versuche im Moment, Geld zu sparen, denn im Oktober werde ich die Miete für meine Studentenwohnung bezahlen müssen.**

(*30 seconds*)

(t) Question number eleven.

Boris tells you there is a festival tomorrow.

What attractions are there? Write **two** things.

(m) **Morgen gibt es ein Kulturfestival in der Stadt. Hunderte alter Segelschiffe kommen zum Fest. Am Abend gibt es Feuerwerk und spanischen Tanz am Rathausplatz. Kommst du mit?**

(*30 seconds*)

(t) Question number twelve.

Jutta tells you about her hotel room.

Which is her room? Tick the correct box.

What is the problem with her room?

(f) **Mein Hotelzimmer ist ziemlich schön. Es gibt ein Einzelbett und einen großen Kleiderschrank. An der Wand gibt es einen modernen Fernseher. Das einzige Problem ist, dass ich das Fenster nicht aufmachen kann.**

(*30 seconds*)

(t) End of test.

Now look over your answers.

[*END OF TRANSCRIPT*]

FOR OFFICIAL USE

G

Total Mark

1300/406

NATIONAL QUALIFICATIONS 2009

WEDNESDAY, 20 MAY
11.55 AM – 12.20 PM
(APPROX)

GERMAN STANDARD GRADE
General Level
Listening

Fill in these boxes and read what is printed below.

Full name of centre

Town

Forename(s)

Surname

Date of birth
Day Month Year

Scottish candidate number

Number of seat

When you are told to do so, open your paper.

You will hear a number of short items in German. You will hear each item three times, then you will have time to write your answer.

Write your answers, **in English**, in this book, in the appropriate spaces.

You may take notes as you are listening to the German, but only in this book.

You may **not** use a German dictionary.

You are not allowed to leave the examination room until the end of the test.

Before leaving the examination room you must give this book to the invigilator. If you do not, you may lose all the marks for this paper.

SA 1300/406 6/11520

DO NOT WRITE IN THIS MARGIN

Marks

You are on holiday in Majorca. You meet two young Germans, Boris and Jutta.

Du bist im Urlaub auf Mallorca. Du triffst zwei junge Deutsche, Boris und Jutta.

1. You chat to Boris about their holiday.

(*a*) Are the statements **True** or **False**? Tick (✓) the correct box for each one. **2**

	True	False
They go to Majorca every year.		
They arrived yesterday.		

(*b*) What does Boris ask you? **1**

____

* * * * *

2. Boris talks about how cheap it is to get to Majorca.

What does he say? Complete the sentence. **1**

A flight to Majorca costs less than ______________________.

* * * * *

3. Jutta tells you that her parents also like Majorca.

Why is Majorca special to them? **1**

____

____

* * * * *

4. Jutta tells you there is a beach nearby.

What does she say about it? Write **three** things. **3**

____

____

____

* * * * *

DO NOT WRITE IN THIS MARGIN

Marks

5. Jutta talks about restaurants.

(*a*) What does she say about the restaurants in town? Tick (✓) **two** boxes. **2**

	Tick
There is a big choice.	
They are open all year.	
The food is cheap.	
The food is delicious.	

(*b*) What type of food does she prefer? Complete the sentence. **1**

She prefers ________________________________ food.

* * * * *

6. Boris talks about his favourite restaurant.

(*a*) Where exactly is the restaurant? Tick (✓) the correct box. **1**

	Tick
In the town centre	
Near the airport	
At the harbour	

(*b*) What is the restaurant's speciality? Complete the sentence. **1**

The restaurant's speciality is ____________________________.

* * * * *

7. Jutta tells you what happened to her during last year's holiday.

What happened? Write **two** things. **2**

____

____

____

* * * * *

DO NOT WRITE IN THIS MARGIN

Marks

8. Boris gives you advice about staying safe in the sun.

What does he say you should do? Write **three** things. **3**

____

____

____

____

* * * * *

9. Jutta tells you she plans to go shopping.

(*a*) What is she going to buy? Tick (✓) the correct box. **1**

Hallo MODE Glanz! ZUSTIMMUNG

☐ ☐ ☐

(*b*) What does she say about the department stores? Complete the sentences. **2**

Most department stores are open ______________________________.

The sales assistants are ______________________________.

* * * * *

10. Boris tells you he doesn't want to go shopping.

Why does he not want to go? Complete the sentence. **1**

He is trying to save money for ______________________________

______________________________.

* * * * *

DO NOT WRITE IN THIS MARGIN

Marks

11. Boris tells you there is a festival tomorrow.

What attractions are there? Write **two** things. **2**

* * * * *

12. Jutta tells you about her hotel room.

(*a*) Which is her room? Tick (✓) the correct box. **1**

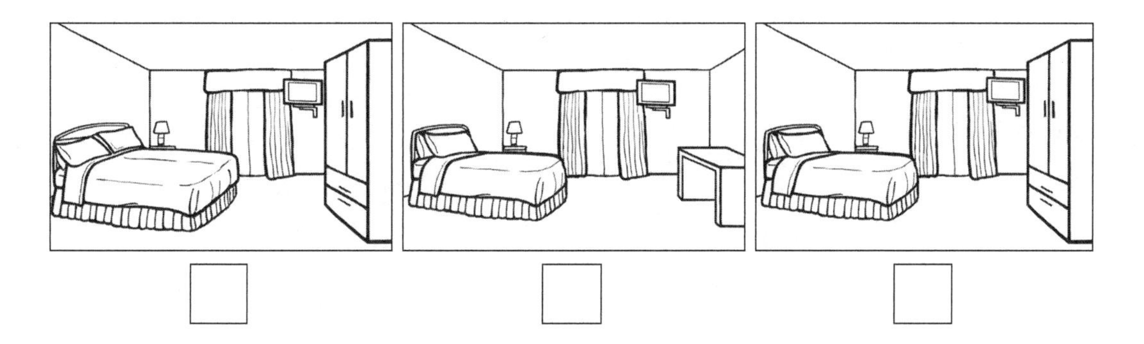

(*b*) What is the problem with her room? **1**

* * * * *

Total (26)

[*END OF QUESTION PAPER*]

[BLANK PAGE]

STANDARD GRADE | CREDIT

2009

[BLANK PAGE]

FOR OFFICIAL USE

C

Total

1300/403

NATIONAL QUALIFICATIONS 2009

WEDNESDAY, 20 MAY
1.30 PM – 2.30 PM

GERMAN STANDARD GRADE
Credit Level
Reading

Fill in these boxes and read what is printed below.

Full name of centre

Town

Forename(s)

Surname

Date of birth
Day Month Year

Scottish candidate number

Number of seat

When you are told to do so, open your paper and write your answers **in English** in the spaces provided.

You may use a German dictionary.

Before leaving the examination room you must give this book to the invigilator. If you do not, you may lose all the marks for this paper.

DO NOT WRITE IN THIS MARGIN

Marks

You are reading a German magazine.

1. This article is about school summer holidays.

Die meisten Schüler freuen sich auf die Sommerferien. Diese bedeuten eine Zeit der Erholung nach den Strapazen eines langen Schuljahres. Es gibt auch die Möglichkeit, längere Zeit mit Freunden oder Verwandten zu verbringen.

Für viele Eltern aber gibt es die alljährliche Frage: Wie kann ich mein Kind während der Sommerferien beschäftigen? Bei schlechtem Wetter und niedrigen Temperaturen ist es besonders schwierig—es ist fast unmöglich, jeden Tag geeignete Aktivitäten für Kinder zu finden.

(*a*) Why do most pupils look forward to the summer holidays? Write **two** things. **2**

____

____

____

(*b*) What problem do parents face at holiday time? **1**

____

____

(*c*) When does this problem become especially difficult? **1**

____

DO NOT WRITE IN THIS MARGIN

Marks

1. (continued)

The article gives ideas for parents with younger children.

Ältere Kinder werden fast immer ihre eigenen Ideen und Einfälle haben, was Freizeit betrifft. Für jüngere Kinder ist es aber oft ein heikles Problem, was man in den Ferien machen soll. Computerspiele sollte man besser vermeiden, weil die Kinder sowieso zu oft vor dem Bildschirm sitzen. Britta Hasek, Direktorin eines Kindergartens in Hannover, hat hier einige Tipps für verzweifelte Eltern: „Eltern sollten sich vor allem mit den Kindern hinsetzen. Wenn sie etwas gemeinsam tun, genießen Kinder die ungeteilte Aufmerksamkeit der Eltern. Alle Kinder brauchen ein Gefühl der Wichtigkeit."

(*d*) Why is it better to avoid computer games when young children are on holiday? **1**

____

____

(*e*) Britta Hasek suggests that parents should do things together with their children.

Why is this good for children? Write **two** things. **2**

____

____

____

[Turn over

DO NOT WRITE IN THIS MARGIN

Marks

2. This article talks about the alcohol problem facing German teenagers.

Alkohol ist nach dem Rauchen die Droge Nummer eins in Deutschland. In Deutschland fangen die Jugendlichen im Durchschnitt im Alter von 14 Jahren an zu trinken, und das ist sehr gefährlich. Wenn man sehr jung ist, ist die Gefahr einer Alkoholvergiftung sehr groß, weil junge Menschen weniger Alkohol vertragen als Erwachsene.

Jugendliche trinken aus unterschiedlichen Motiven—oft machen sie das, weil sie kein Außenseiter in der Gruppe sein wollen. Andere trinken, um die Einsamkeit zu vertreiben.

(*a*) Why is alcohol so dangerous for young people? Write **two** things. **2**

___

___

___

(*b*) What reasons are given for young people drinking? Write **two** things. **2**

___

___

___

Marks

2. (continued)

18-year-old Konrad writes about his experience of alcohol.

Heute trinke ich keinen Alkohol mehr. Meine Probleme begannen kurz nach der Scheidung meiner Eltern. Ich habe Alkohol benutzt, um meine Sorgen loszuwerden. Bald begann ich, fast jeden Tag heimlich Alkohol zu trinken—so war die Welt für mich erträglich.

Eines Tages hat mich ein Lehrer beiseite genommen—er hatte gemerkt, dass meine Noten immer schlechter wurden, und er wollte mir helfen.

(*c*) What made Konrad turn to alcohol? Write **two** things. **2**

(*d*) What alerted his teacher to his problem? **1**

[Turn over

DO NOT WRITE IN THIS MARGIN

Marks

2. **(continued)**

Meine Eltern waren zum Teil Schuld, weil sie nie Familienprobleme mit mir besprochen haben. Mein Lehrer, Herr Ahrends, hat für meine Lage Verständnis gezeigt. Er erkannte die Probleme aus eigener Erfahrung, denn sein Bruder hatte auch zu viel getrunken, als er jung war. Heute bin ich froh, dass ich noch Kontakt zu ihm habe, denn ich weiß, dass er immer für mich da ist, wenn es eine Krise gibt.

(*e*) Why does Konrad think his parents were partly to blame for the problems he had? **1**

____

____

(*f*) Why was Konrad's teacher so understanding? **1**

____

____

(*g*) Konrad is still in touch with his teacher. Why is he pleased about this? **1**

____

____

DO NOT WRITE IN THIS MARGIN

Marks

3. You read an article about taxi driving in Hamburg.

Wenn man neben dem Hauptjob am Wochenende noch arbeiten möchte, hat man nicht so viele Möglichkeiten. Taxifahren ist aber eine ideale Lösung, denn am Wochenende ist Hochkonjunktur. Da kann man recht gut verdienen.

Bevor man sich anmelden kann, muss man eine zweistündige Prüfung bestehen. Man muss beweisen, dass man sich in der Stadt Hamburg gut auskennt. Das ist eine grundsätzliche Voraussetzung für den Job. Dann kommt noch eine ärztliche Untersuchung—man muss ja körperlich fit sein, weil zehn Stunden im Auto viel Ausdauer erfordern.

(*a*) Why is driving a taxi a good idea if you want an extra job at weekends? **1**

____

____

(*b*) Before you can become a taxi driver, you must pass an exam.

What is the exam designed to prove? **1**

____

(*c*) Why must a taxi driver be physically fit? **1**

____

[Turn over

DO NOT WRITE IN THIS MARGIN

Marks

3. (continued)

Paul Niebühler talks about his job as a taxi driver in Hamburg.

Ich bin seit zehn Jahren Taxifahrer in meiner Heimatstadt, Hamburg. Früher habe ich in einer Fabrik gearbeitet, wo ich wirklich nicht schlecht verdient habe. Ich bin aber von Natur aus ein geselliger Mensch und in der Fabrik hatte ich fast keine Gelegenheit, mit meinen Kollegen zu plaudern—das konnte ich nicht ertragen. Mein Schwager musste sein Taxiunternehmen in Hamburg verkaufen, weil er nach Frankfurt ziehen wollte, und das war für mich eine einmalige Chance. Es war nicht einfach, und meine Frau und ich mussten uns Geld von Bekannten leihen, aber es hat sich gelohnt.

(*d*) Why did Paul not like his job in a factory? Write **two** things. **2**

(*e*) How did Paul get the opportunity to become a taxi driver? **1**

DO NOT WRITE IN THIS MARGIN

Marks

3. (continued)

Paul talks about an unusual trip he made.

Die längste Fahrt, die ich gemacht habe, ging von Hamburg nach München —eine Strecke von fast 800 Kilometern. Mein Fahrgast hatte sich in eine Frau aus München verliebt und er wollte ihr einen Heiratsantrag machen. Er hat mir das Essen, das Hotel und 600 Euro für die Fahrt bezahlt. Danach habe ich mich zwei Tage ausgeruht, und ich habe mir gleich versprochen, dass ich das nie wieder machen würde!

(*f*) Why did the passenger want to get to Munich? **1**

____

____

(*g*) What did Paul do after this trip? Write **two** things. **2**

____

____

____

Total (26)

[*END OF QUESTION PAPER*]

[BLANK PAGE]

C

1300/409

NATIONAL QUALIFICATIONS 2009

WEDNESDAY, 20 MAY
2.50 PM – 3.20 PM (APPROX)

GERMAN
STANDARD GRADE
Credit Level
Listening Transcript

This paper must not be seen by any candidate.

The material overleaf is provided for use in an emergency only (eg the recording or equipment proving faulty) or where permission has been given in advance by SQA for the material to be read to candidates with additional support needs. The material must be read exactly as printed.

Transcript—Credit Level

Instructions to reader(s):

For each item, read the English **once**, then read the German **three times**, with an interval of 5 seconds between the readings. On completion of the third reading, pause for the length of time indicated in brackets after each item, to allow the candidates to write their answers.

Where special arrangements have been agreed in advance to allow the reading of the material, those sections marked **(f)** should be read by a female speaker and those marked **(m)** by a male; those sections marked **(t)** should be read by the teacher.

(t) You are spending a week with your pen friend, Peter, in Germany.

(f) or (m) **Du verbringst eine Woche bei deinem Brieffreund, Peter, in Deutschland.**

(t) Question number one.

Peter's mum talks about her work as a travel agent.

Why does she enjoy her work? Write **two** things.

What is the disadvantage of the job?

(f) **Meine Arbeit im Reisebüro gefällt mir gut. Meine Arbeitskollegen sind alle sehr nett, und ich bekomme zehn Prozent Ermäßigung auf alle Reisen. Ich muss aber an sechs Tagen in der Woche arbeiten, und das ist natürlich ärgerlich.**

(*40 seconds*)

(t) Question number two.

Peter's mum has stopped driving to work and now cycles instead.

Why is this? Write **three** things.

(f) **Früher bin ich immer mit dem Auto in die Stadt gefahren, aber seit zwei Monaten fahre ich mit dem Rad. Der Arzt hat es mir empfohlen, weil es viel gesünder ist. Es ist besser für die Umwelt, und ich spare auch etwas Geld, weil Benzin teuer ist.**

(*40 seconds*)

(t) Question number three.

Peter tells you about a book festival in his town.

Why did he enjoy last year's festival? Write **two** things.

(m) **Jedes Jahr findet hier ein Bücherfest statt. Das Fest letztes Jahr war wirklich toll. Wir hatten Autoren aus mehr als zwanzig Ländern, und das fand ich prima. Man hatte auch die Chance, mit den Autoren zu sprechen und Fragen zu stellen.**

(*40 seconds*)

(t) Question number four.

Peter suggests you go to watch a film called "Eisenmann".

Why does he want to see this film? Write **two** things.

(m) **Wollen wir heute Abend ins Kino gehen? Es gibt einen neuen Film, "Eisenmann", den ich unbedingt sehen möchte. Ich interessiere mich sehr für Kriegsfilme. Ich habe die Kritik des Films in der Zeitung gelesen, und er soll spannend sein.**

(*40 seconds*)

(t) Question number five.

Peter's mum does not want him to go to the cinema tonight.

Why is this? Write **two** things.

(f) **Ich finde, dass das Kino keine gute Idee ist, Peter. Du hast schon im Laufe der Woche zu viel Geld ausgegeben, und es ist höchste Zeit, dass du einen Abend zu Hause verbringst. Übrigens solltest du endlich Zeit finden, dein Zimmer aufzuräumen.**

(*40 seconds*)

(t) Question number six.

Peter tells you about Gabriela, a girl in his class who is causing problems.

What problems is she causing? Write **three** things.

(m) **In meiner Klasse haben wir ein Mädchen namens Gabriela. Sie vergisst ständig Hausaufgaben und sie ist oft sehr frech, wenn sie mit den Lehrern spricht. Erst letzte Woche hat sie die Handtasche von einer Lehrerin gestohlen. Wir waren alle ganz erschrocken.**

(*40 seconds*)

(t) Question number seven.

Peter's mum knows Gabriela's background.

How does she know Gabriela's father?

What has made life difficult for Gabriela? Write **two** things.

(f) **Gabriela Fischer ist das, nicht wahr? Ihr Vater und ich hatten einen Ferienjob zusammen in der Bäckerei, als wir jung waren. Gabrielas Bruder ist vor zwei Jahren nach Amerika ausgewandert, und sie vermisst ihn sehr. Dann musste die Familie ihr Haus verkaufen, weil die Mutter ihren Job verloren hatte. Das ist wirklich sehr traurig.**

(*40 seconds*)

[Turn over for Questions 8 to 10 on *Page four*

(t) Question number eight.

Peter gives his opinion on Gabriela's problems.

Why does he have little sympathy for Gabriela?

What lessons should Gabriela learn? Write **two** things.

(m) **Ich habe wenig Mitleid mit Gabriela, denn die Lehrer in der Schule haben versucht, ihr zu helfen, aber sie hört nicht zu. Gabriela muss lernen, dass es andere Leute gibt, die größere Probleme haben. Sie muss verstehen, dass die anderen in der Klasse lernen wollen.**

(*40 seconds*)

(t) Question number nine.

Peter's mum talks about when she was a teenager.

What problems did she have? Write **two** things.

(f) **Als ich jünger war, war das Leben ganz anders als heute. Ich hatte kein Handy, um mit Freunden zu sprechen, und mein Vater schimpfte immer, weil die Telefonrechnung so hoch war. Man konnte die neuesten Filme nicht zu Hause sehen, sondern nur im Kino. Das war natürlich nicht so praktisch.**

(*40 seconds*)

(t) Question number ten.

Peter reminds his mum that teenagers nowadays have problems, too.

What problems does he mention? Write **two** things.

(m) **Ja, du hast Recht, Mama, aber heutzutage ist es auch nicht immer leicht für uns junge Leute. Wir müssen ja immer die richtige Kleidung tragen, um in zu sein. Außerdem ist es schwierig, eine gute Arbeit zu finden, wenn wir von der Schule abgehen.**

(*40 seconds*)

(t) End of test.

Now look over your answers.

[*END OF TRANSCRIPT*]

FOR OFFICIAL USE

C

Total Mark

1300/408

NATIONAL QUALIFICATIONS 2009

WEDNESDAY, 20 MAY
2.50 PM – 3.20 PM (APPROX)

GERMAN STANDARD GRADE
Credit Level
Listening

Fill in these boxes and read what is printed below.

Full name of centre

Town

Forename(s)

Surname

Date of birth
Day Month Year

Scottish candidate number

Number of seat

When you are told to do so, open your paper.

You will hear a number of short items in German. You will hear each item three times, then you will have time to write your answer.

Write your answers, **in English**, in this book, in the appropriate spaces.

You may take notes as you are listening to the German, but only in this book.

You may **not** use a German dictionary.

You are not allowed to leave the examination room until the end of the test.

Before leaving the examination room you must give this book to the invigilator. If you do not, you may lose all the marks for this paper.

DO NOT WRITE IN THIS MARGIN

Marks

You are spending a week with your pen friend, Peter, in Germany.

Du verbringst eine Woche bei deinem Brieffreund, Peter, in Deutschland.

1. Peter's mum talks about her work as a travel agent.

(*a*) Why does she enjoy her work? Write **two** things. 2

(*b*) What is the disadvantage of the job? 1

* * * * *

2. Peter's mum has stopped driving to work and now cycles instead.

Why is this? Write **three** things. 3

* * * * *

3. Peter tells you about a book festival in his town.

Why did he enjoy last year's festival? Write **two** things. 2

* * * * *

DO NOT WRITE IN THIS MARGIN

Marks

4. Peter suggests you go to watch a film called "Eisenmann".

Why does he want to see this film? Write **two** things. **2**

* * * * *

5. Peter's mum does not want him to go to the cinema tonight.

Why is this? Write **two** things. **2**

* * * * *

6. Peter tells you about Gabriela, a girl in his class who is causing problems.

What problems is she causing? Write **three** things. **3**

* * * * *

[Turn over

DO NOT WRITE IN THIS MARGIN

Marks

7. Peter's mum knows Gabriela's background.

(*a*) How does she know Gabriela's father? **1**

(*b*) What has made life difficult for Gabriela? Write **two** things. **2**

* * * * *

8. Peter gives his opinion on Gabriela's problems.

(*a*) Why does he have little sympathy for Gabriela? **1**

(*b*) What lessons should Gabriela learn? Write **two** things. **2**

* * * * *

9. Peter's mum talks about when she was a teenager.

What problems did she have? Write **two** things. **2**

* * * * *

DO NOT WRITE IN THIS MARGIN

Marks

10. Peter reminds his mum that teenagers nowadays have problems, too.

What problems does he mention? Write **two** things. **2**

* * * * *

Total (25)

[*END OF QUESTION PAPER*]

[BLANK PAGE]

STANDARD GRADE | GENERAL

2010

[BLANK PAGE]

FOR OFFICIAL USE

G

Total

1300/402

NATIONAL QUALIFICATIONS 2010

WEDNESDAY, 19 MAY
10.50 AM – 11.35 AM

GERMAN STANDARD GRADE
General Level
Reading

Fill in these boxes and read what is printed below.

Full name of centre

Town

Forename(s)

Surname

Date of birth
Day Month Year

Scottish candidate number

Number of seat

When you are told to do so, open your paper and write your answers **in English** in the spaces provided.

You may use a German dictionary.

Before leaving the examination room you must give this book to the Invigilator. If you do not, you may lose all the marks for this paper.

DO NOT WRITE IN THIS MARGIN

Marks

You are looking at German websites on the Internet.

1. You look at a company's website.

Georg Brauer ist der Besitzer. Man kann ihn jeden Tag in der Fabrik sehen. Er kennt alle Angestellten sehr gut und ist immer guter Laune.

Hans, Sandra und Jörg — unser Verkaufsteam. Sie müssen Schichtarbeit machen und oft geschäftlich ins Ausland reisen.

Karl Jenisch spielt eine wichtige Rolle. Er stellt neue Arbeiter ein.

(*a*) What does it tell you about these people? Complete the sentences. **2**

Georg Brauer knows all the employees and is always ______________

____.

Karl Jenisch is responsible for ______________________________

____.

(*b*) What does the sales team have to do? Write **two** things. **2**

____

____

____

DO NOT WRITE IN THIS MARGIN

Marks

2. Martin writes about seven-a-side rugby.

Vor zwei Jahren hat mein Vater eine Rugbymannschaft in meinem Dorf gegründet. Er hatte die Idee, als er ein Siebener-Rugby Turnier in Schottland gesehen hat.

Siebener-Rugby ist jetzt in Deutschland sehr beliebt. Jedes Spiel dauert nur vierzehn Minuten und man kann ein ganzes Turnier an einem Tag durchführen. So kann man Übernachtungskosten für die Mannschaften sparen.

(*a*) How did Martin's dad get the idea for a seven-a-side rugby team? **1**

____

____

(*b*) Why is seven-a-side rugby so popular in Germany? Write **two** things. **2**

____

____

____

[Turn over

DO NOT WRITE IN THIS MARGIN

Marks

3. In this article, young people write about what they do when they are bored.

Ich gehe in den nächsten Schreibwarenladen und kaufe ein kleines Heft. Dann schreibe ich Gedichte und zeichne ein paar Bilder dazu. Dabei vergeht die Zeit sehr schnell.

Thomas

Wenn mir langweilig ist, räume ich mein Zimmer auf. Manchmal habe ich keine Lust dazu, aber ich fühle mich nachher besser. Das hat auch den Vorteil, dass ich kein Geld ausgeben muss.

Ruth

Weil das Wetter in den letzten Ferien so schlecht war, begann ich, die Geschichte meiner Stadt zu erkunden. Es macht großen Spaß, und ich habe schon viel über die Gegend gelernt.

Hamit

Write the correct name in each box. **4**

Who . . .

	Name
. . . finds out about local history?	
. . . spends time tidying up?	
. . . likes not having to spend money?	
. . . writes and illustrates poems?	

DO NOT WRITE IN THIS MARGIN

Marks

4. You read an interview with Klaus Grimma, a school janitor.

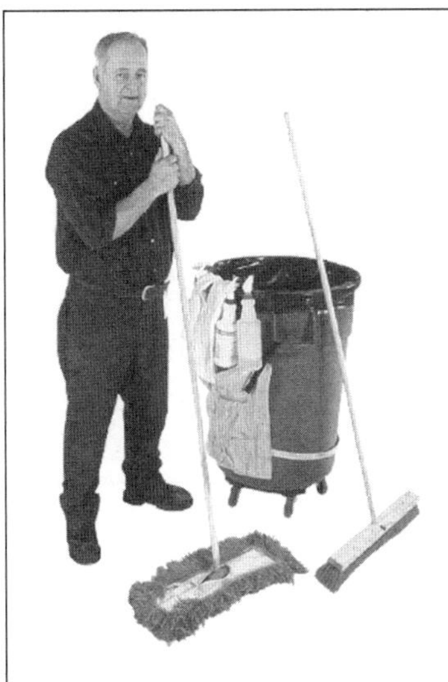

Herr Grimma, seit wann arbeiten Sie als Hausmeister?

Ich bin schon seit 15 Jahren als Hausmeister tätig. Früher war ich zwei Jahre lang Hausmeister in einem Altersheim.

Was machen Sie den ganzen Tag?

Der Job ist sehr abwechslungsreich, aber es gibt auch eine tägliche Routine. Jeden Morgen, bevor die Schüler das Gebäude betreten können, muss ich den Feueralarm prüfen. Jeden Abend, wenn die Schule aus ist, muss ich alle Fenster zumachen.

Macht der Job nach 15 Jahren immer noch Spaß?

Ja, natürlich. Der Job gefällt mir vor allem, weil ich so viele nette junge Leute treffe.

(*a*) Where did Herr Grimma work before becoming a school janitor? **1**

____

(*b*) What does he have to do every morning? **1**

____

(*c*) What does he have to do every evening? **1**

____

(*d*) Why does he enjoy his job so much? **1**

____

____

[Turn over

DO NOT WRITE IN THIS MARGIN

Marks

5. Marc writes about his hobby, fishing.

Zu meinem zehnten Geburtstag habe ich meine erste Angelrute bekommen und seither gehe ich sehr gern angeln. Es gibt einen kleinen Teich in der Nähe von uns, aber das Wasser ist verschmutzt und man kann heutzutage keine Fische mehr fangen. In dem Fluss kann man auch nicht mehr angeln, weil man eine Genehmigung haben muss und das ist recht teuer. Ich kann auch nicht an die Küste fahren, weil das zu weit weg ist.

What problems is Marc having? Complete the sentences. **3**

He cannot catch fish in the pond because ______________________________

____.

He cannot fish ______________________________ because you need a permit.

He cannot fish at the coast because ______________________________.

DO NOT WRITE IN THIS MARGIN

Marks

6. Some young Germans write about Christmas.

Meine drei kleinen Geschwister ärgern mich zu Weihnachten, weil sie zu viel Lärm machen. Zu dieser Jahreszeit denke ich an die Armut und den Krieg auf der Welt.

Sabrina 16

Ich verbringe Weihnachten immer mit meiner Familie zu Hause, aber ich mag das kalte Wetter nicht. Ich möchte lieber Weihnachten auf einer tropischen Insel feiern—vielleicht mit ein paar guten Freunden.

Lars 17

Weihnachten ist gut, wenn alles gut geht. Ich hasse es, in der allerletzten Minute herumzulaufen—die Straßen und Geschäfte sind überfüllt und die Leute sind oft sehr ungeduldig.

Heike 15

Write the correct name in each box. **4**

Who . . .

	Name
. . . would prefer to go away for Christmas?	
. . . finds some members of their family too loud?	
. . . doesn't like the town being busy?	
. . . thinks about poverty and war?	

[Turn over

DO NOT WRITE IN THIS MARGIN

Marks

7. There is an article about a fairytale themed hotel for children.

Das Traumhotel Hänsel und Gretel befindet sich in ruhiger Lage an der deutschen Ostseeküste. Das romantische Hotel lässt Kinderherzen höher schlagen. Die Schlafzimmer sind mit schönen Kindermöbeln ausgestattet. Im Badezimmer nebenan findet man Handtücher mit Märchenfiguren.

Und während die Kinder im Märchenzimmer Spaß haben, genießen die Eltern ein geräumiges Zimmer gleich nebenan. Dieses Zimmer ist nur durch eine Verbindungstür getrennt und hat einen traumhaften Blick auf das Meer.

(*a*) What makes the hotel bedrooms suitable for children? **1**

(*b*) What is special about the towels? **1**

(*c*) Where is the parents' bedroom? **1**

(*d*) What is special about this room? **1**

DO NOT WRITE IN THIS MARGIN

Marks

8. Oya is giving her opinion on family relationships.

Ich komme mit meinen Eltern gut aus, aber mit ihnen kann ich nicht über alles sprechen. Über Themen wie Jungen und Mode kann ich viel besser mit Freundinnen reden. Ich brauche Freiheit, und meine Mutter versteht das besser als mein Vater. Später will ich Kinder haben, aber zur Zeit nicht.

Are the following statements **True** or **False**? Tick (✓) the correct box for each one. **3**

	True	**False**
Oya can speak to her parents about everything.		
Her mum is more understanding than her dad.		
She would like to have children one day.		

[Turn over for Question 9 on *Page ten*

DO NOT WRITE IN THIS MARGIN

Marks

9. This article tells how Jessica, a German girl, came to build a Japanese garden behind her house.

Die Idee für einen japanischen Garten hatte ich, als ich mit der Schule in Japan war. Dort habe ich so viele neue Pflanzen und Blumen gesehen, weil der Vater meiner Gastfamilie, Herr Tashiguro, ein begeisterter Gärtner war.

Einen japanischen Garten hinter meinem Haus in Deutschland zu errichten war aber nicht so einfach. Wir haben nicht besonders viel Platz und das feuchte Wetter in Deutschland ist für exotische Pflanzen nicht geeignet.

Mein Garten ist jetzt ziemlich berühmt, weil ich den ersten Preis in der Landesgartenschau gewonnen habe.

(*a*) Why was Jessica in Japan? **1**

____

(*b*) What inspired her to create her own Japanese garden? **1**

____

____

(*c*) Why was it not easy to build a Japanese garden behind her house in Germany? **1**

____

____

Total (32)

[*END OF QUESTION PAPER*]

G

1300/407

NATIONAL QUALIFICATIONS 2010

WEDNESDAY, 19 MAY
11.55 AM – 12.20 PM
(APPROX)

GERMAN
STANDARD GRADE
General Level
Listening Transcript

This paper must not be seen by any candidate.

The material overleaf is provided for use in an emergency only (eg the recording or equipment proving faulty) or where permission has been given in advance by SQA for the material to be read to candidates with additional support needs. The material must be read exactly as printed.

Transcript—General Level

Instructions to reader(s):

For each item, read the English **once**, then read the German **three times**, with an interval of 5 seconds between the readings. On completion of the third reading, pause for the length of time indicated in brackets after each item, to allow the candidates to write their answers.

Where special arrangements have been agreed in advance to allow the reading of the material, those sections marked **(f)** should be read by a female speaker and those marked **(m)** by a male; those sections marked **(t)** should be read by the teacher.

(t) You are in Bamberg in Germany. You meet Alexander and his sister, Inge.

(f) or (m) **Du bist in Bamberg in Deutschland. Du triffst Alexander und seine Schwester, Inge.**

(t) Question number one.

Alexander asks you some questions.

What does he ask you? Tick **two** boxes.

(m) **Grüß dich! Ich heiße Alexander. Woher kommst du? Wie lange bleibst du hier in Deutschland?**

(30 seconds)

(t) Question number two.

Alexander tells you that there is a lot to do in Bamberg.

What can you do there? Tick **three** boxes.

(m) **Hier in Bamberg gibt es viel zu tun. Man kann in die Eishalle gehen oder eine Schifffahrt machen. Es gibt auch eine Kegelbahn am Stadtrand.**

(30 seconds)

(t) Question number three.

Inge tells you she has pen friends in several countries.

How did she find her first pen friend, Marie? Write **two** things.

(f) **Ein Lehrer in meiner Schule hat zwei Jahre in Frankreich gearbeitet und hat noch viele Freunde da. Er hat mir eine Adresse gegeben.**

(30 seconds)

(t) Question number four.

Inge tells you where Marie lives.

Where exactly is her house? Write **two** things.

(f) **Marie wohnt in einem kleinen Dorf. Sie hat ein schönes Haus neben einer Kirche. Möchtest du ein Foto davon sehen?**

(*30 seconds*)

(t) Question number five.

Inge likes having pen friends.

Why is this? Write **two** things.

(f) **Ich finde es gut, Brieffreunde zu haben. Man lernt viel über ein anderes Land, und es macht Spaß, Briefe zu bekommen.**

(*30 seconds*)

(t) Question number six.

Inge tells you about a time when letters from pen friends were particularly important to her.

What had happened in her life at this time? Write **two** things.

(f) **Vor zwei Jahren sind meine Eltern und ich in eine neue Stadt gezogen. Für mich war das nicht einfach, weil ich am Anfang keine Freunde hatte. Damals waren die Briefe sehr wichtig für mich.**

(*30 seconds*)

(t) Question number seven.

Alexander invites you to a café. He gives you directions.

Where is the café? Tick the correct box on the map.

(m) **Du gehst hier geradeaus, und dann nimmst du die erste Straße links. Das Café ist auf der rechten Seite.**

(*30 seconds*)

(t) Question number eight.

In the café, Alexander tells you about an exchange trip to Scotland.

What went wrong? Tick **three** boxes.

(m) **Mein Schulaustausch nach Schottland war eine Katastrophe. Ich kam mit der Gastfamilie nicht gut aus. In der ersten Woche hatte ich Ohrenschmerzen, und am Ende konnte ich meinen Reisepass nicht finden.**

(*30 seconds*)

[Turn over for Questions 9 to 12 on *Page four*

(t) Question number nine.

Alexander tells you about his pocket money.

When does he get his pocket money?

Why is he unhappy with it? Write **two** things.

(m) **Ich bekomme mein Taschengeld immer am letzten Tag des Monats. Mit dem Taschengeld bin ich gar nicht zufrieden, denn ich muss meine Kleidung selbst kaufen. Alle meine Freunde bekommen viel mehr als ich.**

(30 seconds)

(t) Question number ten.

Inge tells you that she is saving up at the moment.

What is she saving for? Tick the correct box.

How much will it cost? Tick the correct box.

(f) **Ich spare zur Zeit für ein Geburtstagsgeschenk für meine Mutter. Ich habe letzte Woche eine schöne Armbanduhr gesehen. Sie kostet €165.**

(30 seconds)

(t) Question number eleven.

Inge isn't happy with the shops in town.

In which shop do you have to queue for a long time?

What does she **not** like about the department store?

(f) **Ich gehe nicht gern in der Stadt einkaufen. Es gibt eine neue Apotheke, aber da muss man sehr lange warten. Im Kaufhaus haben sie ganz tolle Sachen, aber da ist alles viel zu teuer.**

(30 seconds)

(t) Question number twelve.

Alexander likes the town.

Why does he like going into town? Complete the sentence.

Why is the town centre so pleasant? Tick the correct box.

(m) **Ich gehe gern in die Stadt, denn es ist sehr ruhig dort. Die Stadtmitte ist so angenehm, weil es dort keinen Verkehr gibt.**

(30 seconds)

(t) End of test.

Now look over your answers.

[*END OF TRANSCRIPT*]

FOR OFFICIAL USE

G

Total Mark

1300/406

NATIONAL QUALIFICATIONS 2010

WEDNESDAY, 19 MAY
11.55 AM – 12.20 PM
(APPROX)

GERMAN
STANDARD GRADE
General Level
Listening

Fill in these boxes and read what is printed below.

Full name of centre

Town

Forename(s)

Surname

Date of birth
Day Month Year

Scottish candidate number

Number of seat

When you are told to do so, open your paper.

You will hear a number of short items in German. You will hear each item three times, then you will have time to write your answer.

Write your answers, **in English**, in this book, in the appropriate spaces.

You may take notes as you are listening to the German, but only in this book.

You may **not** use a German dictionary.

You are not allowed to leave the examination room until the end of the test.

Before leaving the examination room you must give this book to the Invigilator. If you do not, you may lose all the marks for this paper.

Marks

You are in Bamberg in Germany. You meet Alexander and his sister, Inge.

Du bist in Bamberg in Deutschland. Du triffst Alexander und seine Schwester, Inge.

1. Alexander asks you some questions.

What does he ask you? Tick (✓) **two** boxes. **2**

	Tick
Where do you come from?	
How did you travel to Germany?	
How long are you staying in Germany?	
How long did the journey take?	

* * * * *

2. Alexander tells you that there is a lot to do in Bamberg.

What can you do there? Tick (✓) **three** boxes. **3**

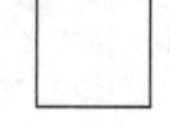

* * * * *

DO NOT WRITE IN THIS MARGIN

Marks

3. Inge tells you she has pen friends in several countries.

How did she find her first pen friend, Marie? Write **two** things. 2

* * * * *

4. Inge tells you where Marie lives.

Where exactly is her house? Write **two** things. 2

* * * * *

5. Inge likes having pen friends.

Why is this? Write **two** things. 2

* * * * *

6. Inge tells you about a time when letters from pen friends were particularly important to her.

What had happened in her life at this time? Write **two** things. 2

* * * * *

[Turn over

DO NOT WRITE IN THIS MARGIN

Marks

7. Alexander invites you to a café. He gives you directions.

Where is the café? Tick (✓) the correct box on the map. **1**

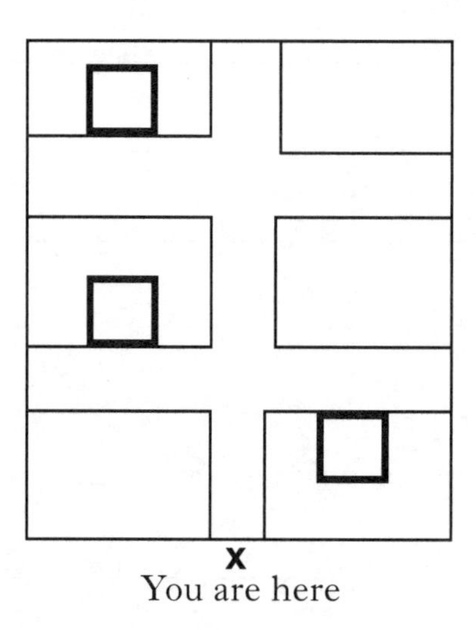

* * * * *

8. In the café, Alexander tells you about an exchange trip to Scotland.

What went wrong? Tick (✓) **three** boxes. **3**

	Tick
He missed his own family.	
He didn't get on with the family in Scotland.	
He had sore ears.	
He had a sore stomach.	
He couldn't find his wallet.	
He couldn't find his passport.	

* * * * *

DO NOT WRITE IN THIS MARGIN

Marks

9. Alexander tells you about his pocket money.

(*a*) When does he get his pocket money? **1**

(*b*) Why is he unhappy with it? Write **two** things. **2**

* * * * *

10. Inge tells you that she is saving up at the moment.

(*a*) What is she saving for? Tick (✓) the correct box. **1**

☐ ☐ ☐

(*b*) How much will it cost? Tick (✓) the correct box. **1**

	Tick
€156	
€160	
€165	

* * * * *

[Turn over for Questions 11 and 12 on *Page six*

DO NOT WRITE IN THIS MARGIN

Marks

11. Inge isn't happy with the shops in town.

(*a*) In which shop do you have to queue for a long time? **1**

____

(*b*) What does she **not** like about the department store? **1**

____

* * * * *

12. Alexander likes the town.

(*a*) Why does he like going into town? Complete the sentence. **1**

He likes going into town because it is very ____________________.

(*b*) Why is the town centre so pleasant? Tick (✓) the correct box. **1**

	Tick
There is no traffic.	
There is no litter.	
There is no air pollution.	

* * * * *

Total (26)

[*END OF QUESTION PAPER*]

STANDARD GRADE | CREDIT

2010

[BLANK PAGE]

FOR OFFICIAL USE

C

Total

1300/403

NATIONAL QUALIFICATIONS 2010

WEDNESDAY, 19 MAY
1.30 PM – 2.30 PM

GERMAN
STANDARD GRADE
Credit Level
Reading

Fill in these boxes and read what is printed below.

Full name of centre

Town

Forename(s)

Surname

Date of birth
Day Month Year

Scottish candidate number

Number of seat

When you are told to do so, open your paper and write your answers **in English** in the spaces provided.

You may use a German dictionary.

Before leaving the examination room you must give this book to the Invigilator. If you do not, you may lose all the marks for this paper.

Marks

1. This magazine article is about teenagers going on holiday without their parents.

Immer mehr Jugendliche wollen die Ferien ohne ihre Eltern verbringen. Viele Eltern werden aber nervös, wenn sie wissen, dass ihre Kinder allein in den Urlaub fahren wollen. „Wenn meine Tochter ins Ausland fahren will mache ich mir Sorgen, weil sie Fremdsprachen nie richtig gelernt hat", sagt Antje Weibers (42) aus Hamburg. Antje versteht aber, warum Jugendliche allein in den Urlaub fahren wollen. „Ich weiß, dass Teenager unabhängig sein wollen, und sie wollen auch lernen, eigene Entscheidungen zu treffen."

(*a*) Why does Antje Weibers worry when her daughter wants to go on holiday abroad? **1**

____

____

(*b*) According to Antje, why do teenagers want to go on holiday without their parents? Write **two** things. **2**

____

____

____

DO NOT WRITE IN THIS MARGIN

Marks

1. (continued)

Eine tolle Alternative zu dem Streit zwischen Eltern und ihren Kindern ist ein Reiseveranstalter, der speziell Reisen für Jugendliche organisiert. „Das finde ich viel besser", sagt Antje. „Diese Reisefirmen wählen ihre Reiseleiter vorsichtig aus, und sind rund um die Uhr erreichbar." Ihre Tochter, Karla, versteht die Sorgen ihrer Mutter sehr gut und sie will ihre Mutter beruhigen. „Bevor ich mit Freunden wegfahre, stelle ich immer zwei wichtige Fragen: Ist der Reiseveranstalter bekannt? Welche Sicherheitsmaßnahmen gibt es?"

(*c*) Why does Antje think it's better if her daughter goes on an organised tour for young people? Write **two** things. 2

____

____

____

(*d*) What does her daughter Karla consider before she books a holiday? Write **two** things. 2

____

____

____

[Turn over

DO NOT WRITE IN THIS MARGIN

Marks

2. In this article, Paul writes about problems in his local park.

„Im Stadtpark gibt es wegen so viel Müll fast keine Besucher mehr." Als ich letztes Jahr diesen Satz in einem Zeitungsartikel gelesen habe, war ich wirklich traurig. Ich bin hier in der Stadt aufgewachsen, und der Park war ein wichtiger Teil meiner Kindheit. Als Kleinkind haben meine Eltern und ich fast jedes Wochenende die Tiere im Park gefüttert. Gleich nachdem ich den Artikel gelesen habe, habe ich meinem Freund Lukas gesagt: „Wir müssen etwas machen, damit es im Park besser wird."

(*a*) What did Paul read about the park that made him sad? **1**

____

____

(*b*) Why is he so fond of the park? Write **two** things. **2**

____

____

____

DO NOT WRITE IN THIS MARGIN

Marks

2. (continued)

Am nächsten Tag sind Lukas und ich zum Park gegangen. Direkt am Eingang war der erste Müllkorb völlig leer und der Inhalt war überall verstreut: Leere Plastikflaschen unter einer Sitzbank und Getränkedosen auf dem Gras. Herr Lehmann, der Parkwächter, hat uns das Problem erklärt: „Bei schönem Wetter ist es besonders schlimm: Die Ruhe wird durch herum rennende Hunde gestört und Kinder werden oft durch Glasscherben im Gras verletzt."

(*c*) What evidence of litter did Paul and Lukas see at the entrance to the park? Write **two** things. **2**

(*d*) According to Herr Lehmann, what problems are there in the park when the weather is good? Write **two** things. **2**

Gleich nach unserem Besuch haben Lukas und ich einen langen Brief an den Stadtrat geschrieben, in dem wir die Probleme im Park deutlich geschildert haben. Wir hatten viele gute Ideen, und jetzt, sechs Monate später, ist es im Park viel besser. Jetzt müssen alle Parkbesucher ihre Hunde an der Leine führen. Es gibt jetzt Videoüberwachung im Park, und wir Schüler gehen zweimal im Monat dahin, um Abfall zu sammeln.

(*e*) What steps have been taken to improve things in the park? Write **three** things. **3**

DO NOT WRITE IN THIS MARGIN

Marks

3. This article is about Jürgen Drechsler who had to give up his dream of becoming a professional footballer.

Fußballprofi werden. Viele Jugendliche haben diesen Traum, denn die besten Spieler sind weltweit berühmt, und man hat auch die Gelegenheit, ein Vermögen zu machen. Nicht viele Jugendliche schaffen es aber, einen Vertrag bei einem Spitzenverein zu bekommen. Jürgen Drechsler (19) aus Marburg hatte diesen Traum fast verwirklicht. „Mit zehn Jahren habe ich angefangen, Fußball in der Schule zu spielen, und mit siebzehn hatte ich einen dreijährigen Juniorvertrag bei FC Bayern München. Dann aber habe ich einen Unfall gehabt, der meine sportliche Karriere abrupt beendet hat. Ein schwerer Werkzeugkasten ist mir aus der Hand gefallen und hat meinen linken Fuß getroffen."

(*a*) Why do many young people dream of becoming a professional footballer? **1**

(*b*) What shows that the football club Bayern München thought Jürgen had talent? **1**

(*c*) Describe the accident that ended Jürgen's career. **1**

DO NOT WRITE IN THIS MARGIN

Marks

3. (continued)

Nach diesem Unfall hatte Jürgen keine Ahnung, dass seine Verletzung so schwer war. Nach einem Jahr aber bekam er von dem Arzt die fürchterliche Nachricht—seine Karriere war zu Ende. Er war ganz deprimiert. „Am Anfang wollte ich den Kontakt mit anderen Menschen vermeiden und ich wollte über meine Fußballkarriere einfach nicht sprechen.“ Mit der Zeit aber, und mit Hilfe von seinem ehemaligen Trainer, Herrn Heinkes, hat Jürgen endlich den Mut gefunden, über seine Zukunft zu reden. „Meine Berufsaussichten waren nicht so rosig, denn ich war als Schüler nicht besonders fleißig und habe die Schule ohne Zeugnis verlassen.“

(*d*) Jürgen was depressed after he learned that his football career was over. How did he act? Write **two** things. **2**

(*e*) Why were his job prospects not good? **1**

[Turn over for Question 3(*f*) on *Page eight*

DO NOT WRITE IN THIS MARGIN

Marks

3. (continued)

Herr Heinkes hatte von der Hilfsorganisation *Bleib am Ball* gehört und er hat Jürgen die Nummer einer Kontaktperson gegeben. Diese Organisation hilft jungen Fußballspielern beim Einstieg in die Arbeitswelt. Jürgen ist sehr froh, dass er die Organisation gefunden hat. „Da habe ich gelernt, dass die richtige Ausbildung sehr wichtig ist. Ich habe auch gelernt, wie man eine Bewerbung schreibt und wie man bei einem Vorstellungsgespräch einen positiven Eindruck macht."

(*f*) What has Jürgen learned from the organisation *Bleib am Ball*? Write **three** things. **3**

____

____

____

____

Total (26)

[*END OF QUESTION PAPER*]

C

1300/409

NATIONAL QUALIFICATIONS 2010

WEDNESDAY, 19 MAY
2.50 PM – 3.20 PM
(APPROX)

GERMAN
STANDARD GRADE
Credit Level
Listening Transcript

This paper must not be seen by any candidate.

The material overleaf is provided for use in an emergency only (eg the recording or equipment proving faulty) or where permission has been given in advance by SQA for the material to be read to candidates with additional support needs. The material must be read exactly as printed.

Transcript—Credit Level

Instructions to reader(s):

For each item, read the English **once**, then read the German **three times**, with an interval of 5 seconds between the readings. On completion of the third reading, pause for the length of time indicated in brackets after each item, to allow the candidates to write their answers.

Where special arrangements have been agreed in advance to allow the reading of the material, those sections marked **(f)** should be read by a female speaker and those marked **(m)** by a male; those sections marked **(t)** should be read by the teacher.

(t) You are visiting your pen friend, Bernd, in Bonn.

(f) or (m) **Du besuchst deinen Brieffreund, Bernd, in Bonn.**

(t) Question number one.

Bernd tells you about his recent stay at a summer camp.

Why did he go to the summer camp?

What did he enjoy about it? Write **two** things.

(m) **Diesen Sommer habe ich zwei Wochen auf einem Ferienlager verbracht. Meine Mutter arbeitet ganztags, und ich hatte keine Lust, allein zu Hause zu bleiben. Es war prima! Ich habe viele Jugendliche in meinem Alter kennen gelernt, und wir hatten jeden Tag ein volles Programm.**

(*40 seconds*)

(t) Question number two.

Bernd tells you what he did at the camp.

What did he do? Write **three** things.

(m) **Am ersten Tag haben alle Teilnehmer eine lange Fahrradtour gemacht, um die Gegend zu sehen. Später in der Woche haben wir einen Bauernhof besucht, und am Anfang der zweiten Woche haben wir verschiedene Wassersportarten ausprobiert.**

(*40 seconds*)

(t) Question number three.

Bernd's mum tells you about a boy called Max, who was also at the camp.

How did Max's family circumstances change last year?

Why did Max decide to stay with his grandmother?

(f) **Der Max war auch da. Sein Vater hat letztes Jahr einen Job im Ausland bekommen. Max ist aber hier geblieben. Er wohnt bei seiner Großmutter in der Stadt, weil er nächstes Jahr wichtige Prüfungen in der Schule hat.**

(*40 seconds*)

(t) Question number four.

Bernd talks about a scheme at his school to help pupils.

Why did the school introduce this scheme?

How does the scheme work?

(m) **In meiner Schule haben wir ein neues System für Schüler, die ihre Probleme nicht mit einem Lehrer besprechen wollen. Diese Schüler können über ihre Probleme und Gefühle in einer E-Mail schreiben. Ein paar Tage später bekommen sie dann eine Antwort.**

(*40 seconds*)

(t) Question number five.

Bernd tells you more about the scheme.

How did the school raise awareness of the scheme in the local area? Write **two** things.

How successful was this?

(m) **Der Schuldirektor hat über das System im Fernsehen gesprochen, und zwei Schüler aus meiner Klasse haben einen Artikel darüber für die Zeitung geschrieben. Bis jetzt haben mehr als vierzig Schulen in der Region dieses System eingeführt.**

(*40 seconds*)

(t) Question number six.

Bernd's mum tells you that her husband is a chef in a hotel.

What are the disadvantages of the job? Write **two** things.

(f) **Mein Mann ist Koch in einem Hotel. Er macht das gern, aber der Job hat auch Nachteile. Wenn die meisten Leute in den Sommermonaten Ferien haben, muss er arbeiten. Er ist oft sehr müde, wenn er nach Hause kommt.**

(*40 seconds*)

(t) Question number seven.

Bernd's mum tells you that a lot of students work in hotels in summer.

Why is this job ideal for students? Write **two** things.

(f) **Viele Studenten arbeiten im Sommer in Hotels. Für sie ist diese Arbeit ideal. Erstens kann man in der Hochsaison viel Geld verdienen. Zweitens kann man oft kostenlos im Hotel essen. Für Studenten ist das natürlich sehr wichtig.**

(*40 seconds*)

[Turn over for Questions 8 to 10 on *Page four*

(t) Question number eight.

Bernd's mum talks about holiday plans.

Where does she hope to go?

What does she hope to do there? Write **two** things.

(f) **Ich möchte so gerne die Oktoberferien in Südeuropa verbringen. Da könnten wir zwei Wochen lang faulenzen und den Arbeitsstress vergessen. Es wird vielleicht auch möglich sein, ein paar Ausflüge zu machen.**

(*40 seconds*)

(t) Question number nine.

Bernd tells his mum that he doesn't want to go on holiday with her and his dad.

Why is this? Write **two** things.

(m) **Ich will nicht mit Papa und dir in den Urlaub fahren. Wir müssen immer die Sehenswürdigkeiten besichtigen, und das interessiert mich nicht. Ihr wollt am Abend nicht ausgehen und das Nachtleben genießen, und wir müssen dann im Hotel bleiben.**

(*40 seconds*)

(t) Question number ten.

Bernd's mum suggests that he could spend the holidays with his grandparents instead.

Why does she think this would be a good idea? Write **three** things.

(f) **Du könntest die Woche bei Oma und Opa verbringen. Du sagst immer, dass Oma viel besser kochen kann als ich. Du kennst viele Jugendliche, die in der Nähe von Oma wohnen, und du wirst dich nie langweilen. Du kannst auch Opa helfen, den Rasen zu mähen.**

(*40 seconds*)

(t) End of test.

Now look over your answers.

[*END OF TRANSCRIPT*]

FOR OFFICIAL USE

C

Total Mark

1300/408

NATIONAL QUALIFICATIONS 2010

WEDNESDAY, 19 MAY 2.50 PM – 3.20 PM (APPROX)

GERMAN STANDARD GRADE
Credit Level
Listening

Fill in these boxes and read what is printed below.

Full name of centre

Town

Forename(s)

Surname

Date of birth

Day Month Year

Scottish candidate number

Number of seat

When you are told to do so, open your paper.

You will hear a number of short items in German. You will hear each item three times, then you will have time to write your answer.

Write your answers, **in English**, in this book, in the appropriate spaces.

You may take notes as you are listening to the German, but only in this book.

You may **not** use a German dictionary.

You are not allowed to leave the examination room until the end of the test.

Before leaving the examination room you must give this book to the Invigilator. If you do not, you may lose all the marks for this paper.

DO NOT WRITE IN THIS MARGIN

Marks

You are visiting your pen friend, Bernd, in Bonn.

Du besuchst deinen Brieffreund, Bernd, in Bonn.

1. Bernd tells you about his recent stay at a summer camp.

(*a*) Why did he go to the summer camp? **1**

(*b*) What did he enjoy about it? Write **two** things. **2**

* * * * *

2. Bernd tells you what he did at the camp.

What did he do? Write **three** things. **3**

* * * * *

3. Bernd's mum tells you about a boy called Max, who was also at the camp.

(*a*) How did Max's family circumstances change last year? **1**

(*b*) Why did Max decide to stay with his grandmother? **1**

* * * * *

Marks

4. Bernd talks about a scheme at his school to help pupils.

(*a*) Why did the school introduce this scheme? **1**

____

____

(*b*) How does the scheme work? **1**

____

____

* * * * *

5. Bernd tells you more about the scheme.

(*a*) How did the school raise awareness of the scheme in the local area? Write **two** things. **2**

____

____

____

(*b*) How successful was this? **1**

____

____

* * * * *

6. Bernd's mum tells you that her husband is a chef in a hotel.

What are the disadvantages of the job? Write **two** things. **2**

____

____

____

* * * * *

[Turn over

DO NOT WRITE IN THIS MARGIN

Marks

7. Bernd's mum tells you that a lot of students work in hotels in summer.

Why is this job ideal for students? Write **two** things. **2**

* * * * *

8. Bernd's mum talks about holiday plans.

(*a*) Where does she hope to go? **1**

(*b*) What does she hope to do there? Write **two** things. **2**

* * * * *

9. Bernd tells his mum that he doesn't want to go on holiday with her and his dad.

Why is this? Write **two** things. **2**

* * * * *

Marks

10. Bernd's mum suggests that he could spend the holidays with his grandparents instead.

Why does she think this would be a good idea? Write **three** things. **3**

* * * * *

Total (25)

[*END OF QUESTION PAPER*]

[BLANK PAGE]

STANDARD GRADE | GENERAL

2011

[BLANK PAGE]

FOR OFFICIAL USE

G

Total

1300/402

NATIONAL QUALIFICATIONS 2011

THURSDAY, 19 MAY
10.50 AM – 11.35 AM

GERMAN
STANDARD GRADE
General Level
Reading

Fill in these boxes and read what is printed below.

Full name of centre

Town

Forename(s)

Surname

Date of birth
Day Month Year

Scottish candidate number

Number of seat

When you are told to do so, open your paper and write your answers **in English** in the spaces provided.

You may use a German dictionary.

Before leaving the examination room you must give this book to the Invigilator. If you do not, you may lose all the marks for this paper.

DO NOT WRITE IN THIS MARGIN

Marks

You are reading a German magazine.

1. These young people are writing about their hopes and plans for the future.

Ich möchte später im Leben eine Geschäftskette eröffnen mit Fokus auf Damenmode.

Jessica

Ich will immer ein gutes Verhältnis zu Familie und Freunden haben.

Amelie

Ich habe alles, was ich will, und ich bin sehr zufrieden.

Nico

Ich will meine Familie und Freunde überreden, gesünder zu leben.

Leia

Write the correct name in each box. **3**

Who . . .

	Name
. . . wants to get on well with family and friends?	
. . . wants to start their own business?	
. . . has everything that they want already?	

DO NOT WRITE IN THIS MARGIN

Marks

2. Jonas is writing about his part-time job in an art gallery.

Mein Job gefällt mir gut. Ich trage keine Uniform, aber meine Kleider müssen schick sein. Ich trage auch ein kleines, silbernes Schild mit meinem Namen.

Die Arbeit ist einfach. Man muss nur aufpassen, dass niemand etwas kaputt macht.

What does he say? Complete the sentences. **3**

The clothes he wears must be ________________________________.

He wears a ____.

He has to watch that ________________________________

____.

[Turn over

DO NOT WRITE IN THIS MARGIN

Marks

3. You see an advert for summer holiday courses for school pupils.

Vom 10. bis zum 20. August bieten wir verschiedene Kurse für Schüler. Unsere Kurse sind geeignet für Schüler, die . . .

. . . Angst vor dem neuen Schuljahr haben.

. . . bessere Noten wollen.

. . . sich während der Ferien langweilen.

(*a*) Why might pupils attend? Mention any **two** things. **2**

____

____

____

The advert continues.

Hier lernen die Schüler, wie man die Zeit besser nutzt. Man lernt auch, dass es wichtig ist, Probleme zu besprechen.

(*b*) What do pupils learn on the course? Write **two** things. **2**

____

____

____

DO NOT WRITE IN THIS MARGIN

Marks

4. A girl called Sophie has written to the magazine problem page about her best friend, Jana.

Kannst du mir bitte helfen? Ich habe eine Freundin, die Jana heißt. Wir kennen uns seit sechs Jahren und sie ist meine beste Freundin—wir haben die gleiche Handschrift, wir gebrauchen die gleichen Worte und wir haben in vielen Dingen den gleichen Geschmack.

Bald muss Jana die Schule wechseln, denn ihr Vater hat eine neue Stelle gefunden. Es ist fürchterlich—ihr neues Haus ist so weit weg! Was soll ich machen?

Sophie (15 Jahre, aus München)

(*a*) What similarities are there between Sophie and Jana? Mention any **two** things. **2**

______

______

______

(*b*) Why is Jana having to change school? **1**

______

______

(*c*) Why is Sophie worried about this? **1**

______

______

[Turn over

Marks

5. You read the reply to Sophie.

Liebe Sophie

Du darfst nicht vergessen: Es ist für Jana viel schlimmer. Sie muss Freunde in einer neuen Umgebung finden.

Es ist heute ganz einfach, in Kontakt zu bleiben—MSN, Webcam, Skype usw. Du kannst auch Jana in den Schulferien besuchen.

Du kannst deine Sorgen nicht vergessen, aber du solltest mehr an die Zukunft denken.

What does the reply say? Tick (✓) **three** boxes. **3**

	Tick
Jana will miss her friends.	
Jana will have to make new friends.	
You can visit Jana in the holidays.	
You can visit Jana at weekends.	
You should remember the good times.	
You should think about the future.	

DO NOT WRITE IN THIS MARGIN

Marks

6. You read an article about unhealthy teenagers in Germany.

Die meisten Teenager treiben zu wenig Sport

55% aller Teenager treiben weniger als zwei Stunden Sport in einer normalen Woche. 24% aller Teenager essen viel zu viel Fett. Nur 13% essen genug Gemüse und nur 16% essen mindestens zwei Portionen Obst am Tag.

Kerstin Leitner, Schuldirektorin in Bonn, hat eine Lösung für ihre Schule gefunden: Ungesundes Essen ist streng verboten.

(*a*) Why are the following percentages mentioned?

Complete the grid. **3**

55% of teenagers	
13% of teenagers	
16% of teenagers	

(*b*) What has Kerstin Leitner done in her school to help with the problem of unhealthy teenagers? **1**

____

____

[Turn over

DO NOT WRITE IN THIS MARGIN

Marks

7. Luise, a German woman, writes about holidays in Britain.

Ich fahre gern und regelmäßig nach Großbritannien. Ich habe nur positive Erfahrungen, und ich finde die Menschen da sehr sympathisch. Es ist natürlich ein Vorteil, dass ich fließend Englisch sprechen kann.

Ich finde es komisch, dass die Autos auf der linken Straßenseite fahren, und ich fahre lieber mit dem Zug. Ich finde die Züge sehr modern und bequem, aber sie sind nicht immer pünktlich.

Luise Hubner, Berlin

Are the following statements **True** or **False**? Tick (✓) the correct box for each one. **4**

	True	False
Luise thinks that British people are very nice.		
Her English is not very good.		
She prefers to travel by train.		
The trains are always on time.		

DO NOT WRITE IN THIS MARGIN

Marks

8. These young Germans are writing about how their families save energy.

Wir schalten elektronische Geräte aus, bevor wir ins Bett gehen. **Karla**

Wenn wir sehr lange an einer Ampel warten, stellt mein Vater den Motor ab. **Sahiba**

Ich dusche mich, um Energie zu sparen. Wir haben keine Badewanne mehr im Haus. **Andi**

Wir benutzen den Geschirrspüler nur, wenn er wirklich voll ist. **Irfan**

How does each person's family save energy? Write **one** thing for each person. **4**

Karla ______________________________

____

Sahiba ______________________________

____

Andi ______________________________

____

Irfan ______________________________

____

[Turn over for Question 9 on *Page ten*

Marks

9. You see an advert for a children's holiday camp.

Im Preis inbegriffen:

- Unterkunft in großen, komfortablen Wohnwagen
- Vollpension mit Frühstücks– und Mittagsbuffet, dreigängiges Abendmenü
- Versicherung
- Schwimmstunden für Anfänger
- Geführte Wanderung im Wald
- Dunkelwanderung mit Taschenlampen

What is included in the price? Tick (✓) **three** boxes. **3**

	Tick
Accommodation in large comfortable tents	
All meals	
Insurance	
Swimming lessons for all abilities	
Mountain walks	
Walks after dark	

Total (32)

[*END OF QUESTION PAPER*]

G

1300/407

NATIONAL QUALIFICATIONS 2011

THURSDAY, 19 MAY
11.55 AM – 12.20 PM
(APPROX)

GERMAN
STANDARD GRADE
General Level
Listening Transcript

This paper must not be seen by any candidate.

The material overleaf is provided for use in an emergency only (eg the recording or equipment proving faulty) or where permission has been given in advance by SQA for the material to be read to candidates with additional support needs. The material must be read exactly as printed.

Transcript—General Level

Instructions to reader(s):

For each item, read the English **once**, then read the German **three times**, with an interval of 5 seconds between the readings. On completion of the third reading, pause for the length of time indicated in brackets after each item, to allow the candidates to write their answers.

Where special arrangements have been agreed in advance to allow the reading of the material, those sections marked **(f)** should be read by a female speaker and those marked **(m)** by a male; those sections marked **(t)** should be read by the teacher.

(t) You are visiting your pen friend, David, in Germany.

(f) or (m) **Du besuchst deinen Brieffreund, David, in Deutschland.**

(t) Question number one.

David's mum collects you from the airport.

Why is David not with her? Write **two** things.

(f) **Es tut mir leid, dass David nicht hier ist. Er macht seine Hausaufgaben. Dann muss er mit dem Hund spazieren gehen.**

(*30 seconds*)

(t) Question number two.

You have to stop off in town on the way home.

What does David's mum have to do? Complete the sentences.

(f) **Wir müssen nur ganz schnell in die Stadt fahren. Ich muss frische Brötchen von der Bäckerei holen, und ich möchte auch beim Friseur einen Termin machen.**

(*30 seconds*)

(t) Question number three.

You arrive at the house. David's mum asks you some questions.

What does she ask you? Tick **two** boxes.

(f) **Bist du müde? Das war sicher eine lange Reise. Hast du Durst? Möchtest du etwas trinken?**

(*30 seconds*)

(t) Question number four.

David tells you about the plans for tomorrow.

What is he doing tomorrow morning?

What is happening in the afternoon? Write **two** things.

(m) **Morgen früh muss ich zum Zahnarzt gehen. Am Nachmittag haben wir eine Grillparty. Da kannst du meine Freunde kennen lernen.**

(30 seconds)

(t) Question number five.

David's mum tells you about a play on Friday afternoon.

What does she say about it? Write **two** things.

(f) **Am Freitagnachmittag gibt es ein Theaterstück im Rathaus. Für Jugendliche unter sechzehn gibt es zwei Karten zum Preis von einer. Wollt ihr hingehen?**

(30 seconds)

(t) Question number six.

You decide to go to the play. David tells you how you will get there.

How will you get there? Tick the correct box.

Why does he not want to go by bus or taxi? Write **one** thing for each.

(m) **Am besten fahren wir mit der Straßenbahn in die Stadt. Man muss immer lange auf den Bus warten, und ein Taxi kann ganz schön teuer sein.**

(30 seconds)

(t) Question number seven.

At the play, David points out a girl he went out with last week.

How does he describe her? Complete the sentences.

(m) **Siehst du das Mädchen da drüben neben der Bühne—mit glatten Haaren, einer Brille und einem kurzen schwarzen Rock?**

(30 seconds)

(t) Question number eight.

David will not be going out with the girl again.

Why is this? Tick **two** boxes.

(m) **Ich gehe mit ihr nie wieder aus. Sie war schlechter Laune und total unhöflich meinen Freunden gegenüber.**

(30 seconds)

[Turn over for Questions 9 to 12 on *Page four*

(t) Question number nine.

David tells you that his parents are divorced.

What does he say? Complete the sentences.

(m) **Meine Eltern sind seit eineinhalb Jahren geschieden. Mein Vater ist wieder verheiratet. Er wohnt jetzt mit seiner neuen Frau in einer anderen Stadt und sie hat zwei kleine Töchter.**

(*30 seconds*)

(t) Question number ten.

The next day, you meet one of David's teachers in town.

What does David like about him? Write **two** things.

(m) **Das war mein Physiklehrer. Ich mag ihn sehr. Er kann alles gut erklären und er organisiert Ausflüge für die Klasse.**

(*30 seconds*)

(t) Question number eleven.

David's mum tells you about a trip to Scotland.

What did she like about Scotland? Tick the correct box.

What did she not like?

(f) **Schottland hat mir gut gefallen—vor allem die wunderschöne Landschaft im Hochland. Leider hat es die ganze Zeit geregnet.**

(*30 seconds*)

(t) Question number twelve.

One morning, David is unwell.

What is wrong with him?

(m) **Ich will heute zu Hause bleiben. Ich habe Bauchschmerzen. Aua, das tut weh.**

(*30 seconds*)

(t) End of test.

Now look over your answers.

[*END OF TRANSCRIPT*]

FOR OFFICIAL USE

G

Total Mark

1300/406

NATIONAL QUALIFICATIONS 2011

THURSDAY, 19 MAY
11.55 AM – 12.20 PM
(APPROX)

GERMAN
STANDARD GRADE
General Level
Listening

Fill in these boxes and read what is printed below.

Full name of centre

Town

Forename(s)

Surname

Date of birth
Day Month Year

Scottish candidate number

Number of seat

When you are told to do so, open your paper.

You will hear a number of short items in German. You will hear each item three times, then you will have time to write your answer.

Write your answers, **in English**, in this book, in the appropriate spaces.

You may take notes as you are listening to the German, but only in this book.

You may **not** use a German dictionary.

You are not allowed to leave the examination room until the end of the test.

Before leaving the examination room you must give this book to the Invigilator. If you do not, you may lose all the marks for this paper.

SA 1300/406 6/7710

DO NOT WRITE IN THIS MARGIN

Marks

You are visiting your pen friend, David, in Germany.

Du besuchst deinen Brieffreund, David, in Deutschland.

1. David's mum collects you from the airport.

Why is David not with her? Write **two** things. 2

____

____

____

* * * * *

2. You have to stop off in town on the way home.

What does David's mum have to do? Complete the sentences. 2

She has to collect something from the ____________________.

She wants to make an appointment at the ____________________.

* * * * *

3. You arrive at the house. David's mum asks you some questions.

What does she ask you? Tick (✓) **two** boxes. 2

	Tick
Are you tired?	
Are you thirsty?	
Do you want something to eat?	
Do you want to phone home?	

* * * * *

DO NOT WRITE IN THIS MARGIN

Marks

4. David tells you about the plans for tomorrow.

(*a*) What is he doing tomorrow morning? **1**

____

(*b*) What is happening in the afternoon? Write **two** things. **2**

____

____

____

* * * * *

5. David's mum tells you about a play on Friday afternoon.

What does she say about it? Write **two** things. **2**

____

____

____

* * * * *

6. You decide to go to the play. David tells you how you will get there.

(*a*) How will you get there? Tick (✓) the correct box. **1**

☐ ☐ ☐

(*b*) Why does he not want to go by bus or taxi? Write **one** thing for each. **2**

Bus	
Taxi	

* * * * *

DO NOT WRITE IN THIS MARGIN

Marks

7. At the play, David points out a girl he went out with last week.

How does he describe her? Complete the sentences. **3**

The girl has ______________________ hair.

She is wearing ______________________ and a black ______________________.

* * * * *

8. David will not be going out with the girl again.

Why is this? Tick (✓) **two** boxes. **2**

She was . . .

	Tick
. . . boring.	
. . . in a bad mood.	
. . . childish.	
. . . impolite.	

* * * * *

9. David tells you that his parents are divorced.

What does he say? Complete the sentences. **2**

His parents have been divorced for ______________________________________.

His dad's new wife has ____.

* * * * *

DO NOT WRITE IN THIS MARGIN

Marks

10. The next day, you meet one of David's teachers in town.

What does David like about him? Write **two** things. **2**

* * * * *

11. David's mum tells you about a trip to Scotland.

(*a*) What did she like about Scotland? Tick (✓) the correct box. **1**

WHISKY

☐ ☐ ☐

(*b*) What did she not like? **1**

* * * * *

12. One morning, David is unwell.

What is wrong with him? **1**

* * * * *

Total (26)

[*END OF QUESTION PAPER*]

[BLANK PAGE]

STANDARD GRADE | CREDIT

2011

[BLANK PAGE]

FOR OFFICIAL USE

C

Total

1300/403

NATIONAL QUALIFICATIONS 2011

THURSDAY, 19 MAY
1.30 PM – 2.30 PM

GERMAN
STANDARD GRADE
Credit Level
Reading

Fill in these boxes and read what is printed below.

Full name of centre

Town

Forename(s)

Surname

Date of birth
Day Month Year

Scottish candidate number

Number of seat

When you are told to do so, open your paper and write your answers **in English** in the spaces provided.

You may use a German dictionary.

Before leaving the examination room you must give this book to the Invigilator. If you do not, you may lose all the marks for this paper.

DO NOT WRITE IN THIS MARGIN

Marks

You are reading a German magazine.

1. This article is about taking a gap year – a year out between school and university.

Die Entscheidung, ein freies Jahr zwischen Schule und Universität zu haben, gewinnt immer mehr an Popularität. Fast ein Viertel aller Studenten in Deutschland haben das letztes Jahr gemacht.

Viele Jugendliche verbringen das Jahr in einem anderen Land. Es gibt viele Gründe für ein Jahr im Ausland: Man hat etwas Zeit für Entspannung nach den Prüfungen. Für viele Jugendliche ist das Auslandsjahr endlich die Chance, ein großes Abenteuer zu erleben. Es ist auch manchmal die erste Arbeitserfahrung, weil man in der Schulzeit keine Zeit für einen Nebenjob hatte.

(*a*) What statistic shows that taking a gap year is popular with students in Germany? **1**

____

____

(*b*) Why do many young people spend their gap year abroad? Mention **three** things. **3**

____

____

____

____

DO NOT WRITE IN THIS MARGIN

Marks

1. (continued)

Wenn man für das Jahr im Ausland einen Job finden will, gibt es jede Menge Optionen, die man im Internet, in Magazinen oder in der Schule finden kann: Arbeit in einem Seniorenheim in Peru, Obstpflücken in Kanada oder ein Job in einer Schule für behinderte Kinder in Indien. Es gibt viele Arbeitsmöglichkeiten in Frankreich, Spanien und Italien, aber viele Jugendliche wollen außerhalb Europas arbeiten. Das ist aber schwierig, weil eine Arbeitserlaubnis oft erforderlich ist.

(*c*) The article mentions job opportunities abroad. What examples are given? Mention any **two** things. **2**

____

____

____

(*d*) Why is it often difficult to work outside Europe? **1**

____

____

[Turn over

DO NOT WRITE IN THIS MARGIN

Marks

2. There is an article about the 100th anniversary of German youth hostels.

100 Jahre Jugendherbergen

Am 26. August 1909 hat der Lehrer Richard Schirrmann aus Altena einen achttägigen Ausflug mit seiner Schulklasse gemacht. An einem Abend waren sie mitten auf dem Lande und plötzlich begann ein schweres Gewitter. Herr Schirrmann musste mit seinen Schülern in einer kleinen Dorfschule übernachten. Da bekam er die Idee, eine billige Unterkunft für alle jungen Menschen zu schaffen.

Schirrmann hat dann im Jahre 1912 die erste Jugendherberge der Welt in Altena gegründet. Er wollte vor allem Freundschaft und Toleranz unter Jugendlichen fördern.

(*a*) What happened when Richard Schirrmann and his pupils were on a trip in the countryside in 1909? Mention **two** things. **2**

____

____

____

(*b*) What exactly did Schirrmann hope to achieve when he opened the first ever youth hostel in 1912? **1**

____

____

Marks

2. (continued)

This section of the article describes how the anniversary will be celebrated.

> Das Deutsche Jugendherbergswerk (DJH) hat Aktionen und Feste im ganzen Land organisiert.
>
> Eine große Aktion mit dem Titel „100 Jahre–100 Bäume" zeigt die Wichtigkeit der Umwelt in Deutschland.
>
> Am 13. August geben sie eine Sonderbriefmarke und eine Münze zum Jubiläum „100 Jahre Jugendherbergen" heraus.
>
> Und vom 18. bis 26. Juli gibt es in der Stadt Detmold eine Jugendbegegnung – hier können Jugendliche aus ganz Deutschland junge Leute aus anderen Ländern treffen.

(*c*) What is the project "100 years–100 trees" intended to show? **1**

____

____

(*d*) What is happening on the 13th of August? **1**

____

____

(*e*) What will young Germans have the opportunity to do in Detmold in July? **1**

____

____

[Turn over

DO NOT WRITE IN THIS MARGIN

Marks

2. (continued)

Marlene Hubner, a 70-year-old woman, writes about a stay in a youth hostel when she was younger.

Im Jahr 1959 bin ich mit einer Mädchengruppe der Kirche nach Bayern gefahren. Dort sind wir in einer kleinen Jugendherberge in einem Dorf geblieben. Das Leben dort war sehr einfach: Das Wasser mussten wir von dem Brunnen vor dem Haus holen, und für die jungen Gäste gab es nur eine Schaukel im Garten.

Trotz dieser Schwierigkeiten habe ich mich sehr gut amüsiert, denn dort hatte ich zum ersten Mal die Gelegenheit, die Berge kennen zu lernen.

(*f*) Marlene says that the facilities at the hostel were basic. What examples does she give? Write **two** things. **2**

____

____

____

(*g*) Why did Marlene enjoy her trip? **1**

____

____

DO NOT WRITE IN THIS MARGIN

Marks

3. Ferdia and Mae, two German girls, went on a kayak trip in Russia. After the trip, Ferdia wrote this report for the magazine.

Am Anfang des Jahres beschlossen wir, Russland mit dem Paddelboot zu befahren. Vor der Reise hat Mae viele Reiseführer gelesen, während ich die Kultur des Landes studiert habe. Die Vorbereitung dauerte etwa sechs Monate, und wir sind dann am Anfang der Sommerferien nach Russland gefahren – zwei Mädchen, zwei Kajaks und ein Auto. Wir hatten keine Angst, aber mein Vater war nicht so begeistert: Das Auto war nicht besonders zuverlässig, und die Straßen in Russland waren nicht so gut wie in Deutschland.

(*a*) How did Ferdia and Mae prepare for the trip? Mention **two** things. **2**

____

____

____

(*b*) Why was Ferdia's father not keen for the girls to go on the trip? Mention **two** things. **2**

____

____

____

[Turn over

Marks

3. (continued)

> Wir haben 14 Tage auf dem Fluss Nerl verbracht, etwa 150 Kilometer nordöstlich von Moskau. Es gibt keine großen Städte und man kann die Natur richtig genießen. Ich muss aber sagen, dass es ein paar Probleme gibt. Erstens die Mücken! Es gibt so viele Mücken im Sommer, das ist eine Plage. Zweitens ist es ganz schwierig, Holz für das Feuer zu finden. Es gibt auch fast keine Geschäfte und man muss viele Lebensmittel im Kajak mitnehmen.

(*c*) What problems did the girls have on their trip along the river Nerl? Mention **three** things. **3**

____

____

____

____

DO NOT WRITE IN THIS MARGIN

Marks

3. (continued)

Kanusport ist wohl die schönste Art und Weise, eine neue Gegend kennen zu lernen. Es gibt aber in Russland nicht so viele Leute, die Kanu oder Kajak fahren. Das liegt daran, dass die Ausrüstung für Kanufahrer in Russland einfach zu viel Geld kostet, und sogar die Preise für die Vermietung eines Kajaks sind viel zu hoch. Es gibt viele Flüsse und Seen, wo das Kanufahren verboten ist – man darf die Wasservögel nicht stören.

(*d*) Why are there not many canoeists in Russia? Mention **two** things. **2**

____

____

____

(*e*) Why is canoeing forbidden on many Russian rivers and lakes? **1**

____

____

Total (26)

[*END OF QUESTION PAPER*]

[BLANK PAGE]

C

1300/409

NATIONAL QUALIFICATIONS 2011

THURSDAY, 19 MAY
2.50 PM – 3.20 PM
(APPROX)

GERMAN
STANDARD GRADE
Credit Level
Listening Transcript

This paper must not be seen by any candidate.

The material overleaf is provided for use in an emergency only (eg the recording or equipment proving faulty) or where permission has been given in advance by SQA for the material to be read to candidates with additional support needs. The material must be read exactly as printed.

Transcript—Credit Level

Instructions to reader(s):

For each item, read the English **once**, then read the German **three times**, with an interval of 5 seconds between the readings. On completion of the third reading, pause for the length of time indicated in brackets after each item, to allow the candidates to write their answers.

Where special arrangements have been agreed in advance to allow the reading of the material, those sections marked **(f)** should be read by a female speaker and those marked **(m)** by a male; those sections marked **(t)** should be read by the teacher.

(t) You are visiting your exchange partner, Frieda, and her family in Germany.

(f) or (m) **Du besuchst deine Austauschpartnerin, Frieda, und ihre Familie in Deutschland.**

(t) Question number one.

Frieda tells you that she and her friends are going on holiday this summer.

What exactly are they going to do?

Why are they looking forward to this trip? Write **two** things.

(f) **Diesen Sommer werde ich mit Freunden wegfahren. Wir werden eine Bahnreise durch ganz Europa machen. Wir freuen uns sehr darauf, weil man so viel Freiheit hat. Wenn eine Stadt nicht so schön ist, kann man zur nächsten Stadt fahren.**

(40 seconds)

(t) Question number two.

Frieda tells you about a disastrous school trip to Spain.

What went wrong? Write **three** things.

(f) **Unsere Schülerreise war eine Katastrophe. Wir sind nach Spanien geflogen, und das Flugzeug musste in Frankreich landen, weil ein älterer Mann krank war. Wir kamen dann mit fünf Stunden Verspätung in Spanien an.**

(40 seconds)

(t) Question number three.

Frieda's brother, Lukas, explains that their dad won't be going on holiday with the family this year.

Why will he have to stay and work?

What jobs will he have to do? Write **two** things.

(m) **Dieses Jahr kann mein Vater leider nicht mit der Familie in den Urlaub fahren. Er muss hier bleiben, denn seine Firma eröffnet ein neues Büro in der Stadt. Er muss neue Möbel für das Büro kaufen und er muss auch zwei neue Sekretärinnen oder Sekretäre finden.**

(40 seconds)

(t) Question number four.

Frieda complains about her dad working all the time.

Why does she think this is unfair on her mum and the rest of the family? Write **two** things.

(f) **Mein Vater sollte auch mal an uns denken. Letzten Sommer mussten wir alle zu Hause bleiben, weil er arbeiten musste. Auch meine Mutter arbeitet ganztags und sie braucht zwei Wochen Erholung mit gutem Wetter.**

(40 seconds)

(t) Question number five.

Lukas tells you that he has to catch up on a lot of school work.

Why did he miss two weeks of school?

What problem is all this school work causing?

(m) **Ich war zwei Wochen lang nicht in der Schule, weil ich die Grippe hatte. Jetzt muss ich so viel für die Schule machen, dass ich am Abend keine Freizeit habe. Es ist furchtbar!**

(40 seconds)

(t) Question number six.

Frieda wants to go and see a TV chef in the shopping centre tomorrow.

Why does she like this chef? Write **three** things.

(f) **Der Fernsehkoch Tim Mälzer wird morgen im Einkaufszentrum sein. Durch seine Sendungen habe ich so viel gelernt, weil er alles so einfach macht. Er hat einen guten Sinn für Humor, und seine Kochshows sind immer sehr lustig.**

(40 seconds)

(t) Question number seven.

You talk about television.

What do some of Lukas' classmates do?

According to Lukas, what does this say about them?

(m) **Ich kenne ein paar Leute in meiner Klasse, die Fernsehsendungen auf ihrem Handy anschauen. Ich glaube, für sie ist das Fernsehen wichtiger als der Kontakt zu ihren Freunden.**

(40 seconds)

[Turn over for Questions 8 to 10 on *Page four*

(t) Question number eight.

Lukas tells you that he plays in a band.

How do they earn money?

Why are they saving the money?

(m) **Ich spiele Bass in einer Band. Wir spielen jeden Samstagabend in einer Kneipe und wir verdienen dadurch ziemlich viel Geld. Wir sparen das Geld, weil wir dringend bessere Instrumente brauchen.**

(*40 seconds*)

(t) Question number nine.

Lukas tells you about a charity gig.

When is the gig taking place?

What does the organisation "Kinderherz" do?

(m) **Am dreißigsten Mai spielt die Gruppe bei einem Benefizkonzert im Jugendzentrum. Wir wollen Geld für die Organisation "Kinderherz" sammeln. Sie hilft Jugendlichen, die auf der Straße schlafen müssen.**

(*40 seconds*)

(t) Question number ten.

Frieda and her friends will be helping out at the gig.

What will they be doing? Write **three** things.

(f) **Ja, das Konzert wird toll sein. Meine Freunde und ich werden vor dem Konzert Eintrittskarten verkaufen. In der Pause werden wir Getränke servieren, und am Ende werden wir helfen, alles wieder aufzuräumen.**

(*40 seconds*)

(t) End of test.

Now look over your answers.

[*END OF TRANSCRIPT*]

FOR OFFICIAL USE

C

Total Mark

1300/408

NATIONAL QUALIFICATIONS 2011

THURSDAY, 19 MAY
2.50 PM – 3.20 PM
(APPROX)

GERMAN
STANDARD GRADE
Credit Level
Listening

Fill in these boxes and read what is printed below.

Full name of centre

Town

Forename(s)

Surname

Date of birth
Day Month Year

Scottish candidate number

Number of seat

When you are told to do so, open your paper.

You will hear a number of short items in German. You will hear each item three times, then you will have time to write your answer.

Write your answers, **in English**, in this book, in the appropriate spaces.

You may take notes as you are listening to the German, but only in this book.

You may **not** use a German dictionary.

You are not allowed to leave the examination room until the end of the test.

Before leaving the examination room you must give this book to the Invigilator. If you do not, you may lose all the marks for this paper.

DO NOT WRITE IN THIS MARGIN

Marks

You are visiting your exchange partner, Frieda, and her family in Germany.

Du besuchst deine Austauschpartnerin, Frieda, und ihre Familie in Deutschland.

1. Frieda tells you that she and her friends are going on holiday this summer.

(*a*) What exactly are they going to do? **1**

(*b*) Why are they looking forward to this trip? Write **two** things. **2**

* * * * *

2. Frieda tells you about a disastrous school trip to Spain.

What went wrong? Write **three** things. **3**

* * * * *

3. Frieda's brother, Lukas, explains that their dad won't be going on holiday with the family this year.

(*a*) Why will he have to stay and work? **1**

(*b*) What jobs will he have to do? Write **two** things. **2**

* * * * *

DO NOT WRITE IN THIS MARGIN

Marks

4. Frieda complains about her dad working all the time.

Why does she think this is unfair on her mum and the rest of the family? Write **two** things. **2**

* * * * *

5. Lukas tells you that he has to catch up on a lot of school work.

(*a*) Why did he miss two weeks of school? **1**

(*b*) What problem is all this school work causing? **1**

* * * * *

6. Frieda wants to go and see a TV chef in the shopping centre tomorrow.

Why does she like this chef? Write **three** things. **3**

* * * * *

[Turn over

DO NOT WRITE IN THIS MARGIN

Marks

7. You talk about television.

(*a*) What do some of Lukas' classmates do? **1**

(*b*) According to Lukas, what does this say about them? **1**

* * * * *

8. Lukas tells you that he plays in a band.

(*a*) How do they earn money? **1**

(*b*) Why are they saving the money? **1**

* * * * *

9. Lukas tells you about a charity gig.

(*a*) When is the gig taking place? **1**

(*b*) What does the organisation "Kinderherz" do? **1**

* * * * *

DO NOT WRITE IN THIS MARGIN

Marks

10. Frieda and her friends will be helping out at the gig.

What will they be doing? Write **three** things. **3**

* * * * *

Total (25)

[END OF QUESTION PAPER]

Acknowledgements

Permission has been sought from all relevant copyright holders and Bright Red Publishing is grateful for the use of the following:
A logo © Das Deutsche Jugendherbergswerk (2011 Credit Reading page 4).

STANDARD GRADE | ANSWER SECTION

BrightRED ANSWER SECTION FOR

SQA STANDARD GRADE GENERAL AND CREDIT GERMAN 2007–2011

GERMAN GENERAL READING 2007

1. (Holiday traffic) B
(Foreign politicians) E
(New exhibition) D
(World record) A
(Criminals arrested) C

2. (Long lie) Barbara
(House) Kemal
(Car) Katharina
(Holiday) Anne

3. Julia
- Has no friends in her class/Her friends are not in her class
- Sits/stays at home/in the house/goes home/Watches television/TV.

Arno
- (Always) gets bad marks/grades/ Doesn't want to go to school/Has no interest in going to school/Doesn't feel like going to school/Has no desire to go to school/Has no joy/fun/pleasure going to school/Has no time for school/Doesn't like (going to) school/No motivation to go to school/Doesn't enjoy the class
- Meets (a few) friend(s) in town/Goes into town to meet friends/Spends the day in town with friends/Spends the day at/goes to/hangs about at the pedestrian precinct.

Michael
- History teacher is (too) strict/Is scared of history teacher/History teacher frightens him.
- Goes to the harbour/docks/Watches ships/boats.

4. (Nationality) Maria
(Sex) Theresa
(Age) Manfred
(Lack of disabled access) Peter

5. (*a*) (Parents) Tina
(Bowling) Gabi
(*b*) His mother/mum won the tickets/His mum got the tickets in a competition/His mum entered a competition.
(*c*) It's exciting/thrilling/He enjoys the thrill

6. (*a*) (Holidays only) Jelena
(Two days a week) Lara
(Evenings) Thomas
(*b*) Lara
- Sells flowers/blooms/Florist/Has contact with tourists/people from other/different countries/lands/foreigners.
- Has contact with tourists from other/different countries/lands/foreigners/She is studying/learning/when she studies/learns languages.

Thomas
- Gives swimming lessons/Teaches people/children/ young people/teenagers to swim/Helps people/children/young people/teenagers to learn to swim.
- Has learned/is learning (a lot) about working with young people/children/Wants to become/be a PE/sports teacher.

Jelena
- Sells programmes/programme books/booklets
- Wants to become/be an actress/actor/be in plays/on stage.

7. (*a*) *Any two of:*
- Goes to the hairdresser/gets hair done/cut/regularly /a lot/often
- Tries to eat/eats healthy (food).
- Watches/maintains/keeps his figure.

(*b*)
- Smoke.
- (At least) 3 times a week.
- Sleep for 8 hours (a day/night).

GERMAN GENERAL LISTENING 2007

1. Box 1 – bread, cheese, sausage and coffee.

2. top right-hand side box.

3. *Any two of:*
- His brother/he listens to/plays/puts on/has (loud) music (when Martin/he is doing his homework/study).
- He cannot concentrate on his homework/study
- His brother/he takes/borrows/uses/steals his things/stuff/belongings/books/CDs/His things etc go missing.

4. (1st lesson) Chemistry
(2nd lesson) Geography

5. Ticks at:
- Box 2 – how long does each lesson last?
- Box 4 – what do you do at break time?
- Box 5 – what do you think of German?

6. *Any two of:*
- He/we (only) has/have five classes/lessons/ periods/units/blocks (at school)/School ends after period 5.
- School finishes at 12.00/midday
- (In the afternoons) he goes into town/city/down the town/street with his friend(s)/he meets his friend(s) in town/the city (and that is fun).

7. *Any two of:*
- Usually mother/mum/she cooks/Mother/mum/ she doesn't cook
- (On Friday) Martin/he and his brother(s)/her sons/the boys/the brothers cook.
- (On Friday) they do not eat/sit in the dining room/Usually they eat/sit in the dining room.
- (On Friday) they eat/sit/have their meal in front of the television/in the living room/they have a TV dinner.

8. (*a*) *Any one of:*
- rain(y)/wet/showery
- (quite/very/extremely) cold

(*b*) *Any two of:*
- (Go to) ice rink/(ice) skating
- (Visit/go to) (town) museum.
- Write postcard(s).

9. (*a*) Ticks at:
- Box 1 – good pay
- Box 3 – travelling abroad.

(*b*) He (often) has to work nights/at night/ nightshift.

10.
- He has (lots of good) idea(s) for/about/of (new) game(s).
- He writes/wrote (article(s)) about computers for the school/pupils (newspaper/magazine)

11. *Any one of:*
- You sit/work/are/stare at/in front of computer/it/them for hours/for a long time/all the time.
- It is unhealthy/not good for you/for your body.
- It is not good/bad for your eyes/(The brightness) goes for your eyes/It damages your eyes.

12. (Petra's family lives in the town centre) - False.
(They have a garden) - False.

13. Funny/amusing
Fashion/clothes/style

GERMAN CREDIT READING 2007

1. (*a*) *Any two of:*
- A (new) challenge/(More of a) challenge/It's (more) challenging/Feel challenged
  It makes new demands.
- More free time/spare time/time to themselves/ leisure time/time off.
- Move to/live in/go to/be in/work in a new/ different area/town/place/neighbourhood/ district/part of town/region/Change the area etc they're in.

(*b*) *Any two of:*
- He had been/was unemployed/on the dole for 3 months/He hadn't had a job/been working for 3 months/He was between jobs for 3 months.
- His wife (only) had a part-time job/worked part-time.
- (He has/they have/because of) two young children/kids.

(*c*) How demanding/tiring/exhausting/strenuous/ straining it is/how much of an effort it is/ demanding/tiring etc sitting/working at a computer for 7 hours a day/all day/the whole day/putting names and addresses/things into a computer/stuffing (things into) envelopes.

(*d*) *Any two of:*
- (After 3 weeks) he became depressed/it was depressing.
- He didn't want to leave the house/go out/He wanted to stay at home.
- His family (life) began to suffer/go under.

2. (*a*) *Any three of:*
- He is bi-lingual/His mother is German/He is half German.
- He wanted to study chemistry with sport/PE and you cannot do that in Scotland/here/He couldn't do the course/subject(s) he wanted in Scotland/here.
- He has relative(s)/relation(s)/family/aunt(ie) in Heidelberg/Germany/there (and they had a room free).
- The university is old and famous.

(*b*)
- (German) pupils are used to/have a different school system/There is a different school system (in Germany)/German schools have a different system
- Pupils/students in Germany are (often a few/a couple of/one or two years) older (when they begin studying.)/He'll be younger than the German students

(*c*) He might be/gets/is homesick.

(*d*) *Any two of:*
- Things were/it/student life/Germany was more expensive than he had thought/expected.
- He had never learned/had to learn how to deal with/handle/use/manage/what to do with money/it/how to budget/He had no skill with money/it.
- He had always (just) gone/always went to his parents (when he needed something)/when he was broke/His parents gave him money when he asked for it.

(*e*) His parents put/transferred/paid money into his bank/account every month.

(*f*) Budget/plan for a (whole) month/Make a monthly plan/Make the money last the whole month.

3. (*a*) She was doing (2/3 weeks) work experience/a work placement/She was working in a retirement/old folks' home/with old/elderly people (for 2/3 weeks).

(*b*) *Any two of:*
- The family/people she was staying with/host family/guest family was/were taking part/in it.
- Famine/hunger/starvation in Africa (is a(n) disgrace/shame/scandal/problem/issue).
- It is important for the younger generation to make their feelings known/show their feelings.

- It cannot go on/We have to do something/get involved/We have to put a stop to poverty/it.

(*c*) Other Swiss people/another Swiss person were/ was taking part/protesting/She met other Swiss people.

(*d*) *Any two of:*
- The atmosphere/it/mood was (quite) relaxed/ chilled out/laid back.
- The music/musical accompaniment was great/ super.
- She heard a pipe band/group/the pipes/a piper for the first time.

(*e*) The mother of the family she was staying with/host mother/guest family mother had to work/She got the ticket belonging to the mother of the family she was staying with/The mother of the family she was staying with gave her her ticket.

(*f*) It rained (almost all evening/day)/It began to rain.

(*g*) Reminded the politicians of their responsibility/ Made the politicians answer for their actions/Held the politicians responsible.

GERMAN CREDIT LISTENING 2007

1.
- She was/heard it on holiday (with her friend Lisa)/She was on a campsite/camping place/went camping.
- The people in the next tent/next to/near/opposite them played the CD/music/People/someone played the CD/music all day/all the time/the whole time/non-stop

2. (*a*) In the Christmas holidays/At Christmas/Last Christmas

(*b*)
- The tickets/they/the concerts/the tour/it was/ were sold out within/in/after two/2 days/on the second day/The tickets were only on sale for two/2 days.
- There were (over) 2 000 (spectators/people) at each/every concert/all concerts.

3. (*a*) Her sister broke her leg/Her mum/she had to take sister to hospital.

(*b*) By train/rail.

4. *Any three of:*
- 10 pupils/people in her class are learning/play/ know an instrument.
- (Around) 80 (pupils/children/boys and girls/people) (play) in the orchestra/orchester (school) band.
- That is a lot more than in other schools/It's more popular than in other schools/There are more taking the subject than in other schools.
- The choir won first prize in a (national) competition/won a (national) competition (this year).

5.
- It's too hot/warm to sit/be in a/the bus/for two hours/It's too hot and there's no air conditioning/ fresh air.
- Everything (in Germany) has become (so) expensive/It's (so/too) expensive to stay in Germany/Bus tours have become (so) expensive/It's (so) expensive

6.
- It is fun to learn about/he learns about/he likes the history of Frankfurt/the town.
- He meets tourists/(new) people from all over(the world)/around the world/other countries/lands/ different/other places/He meets foreign people/tourists.
- He has (had) famous/well-known sportsmen/sports people/musicians/people/celebrities on his bus.

7. (*a*) 1995/12 years ago

(*b*)
- They/we drive on the left-hand/other/opposite/ different/wrong side/He found it difficult to stay on the left/right side of the road.
- (The people had a strong) accent.

8. (*a*) Guesthouse/Bed & Breakfast/B&B/boarding house/small hotel/small inn

(*b*) *Any two of:*
- Central/Centre/middle of town/city/(Quite) near centre of town.
- Five minutes from the river.
- Lots of wine bars/wine drinking places (nearby).

9. *Any two of:*
- In summer there are (too) many/lots of buses/There are too many tour/holiday/tourist buses/buses with/for tourists.
- The streets are (too) narrow/small/tight (for the buses)/ The buses are too big for the streets.
- It can be dangerous/not safe for children and the elderly.

10.
- Rüdesheim/the area needs the tourists and the money they bring/Tourism/tourists bring(s) money/is/are good for the economy.
- (If the town is full of tourists,) the shops and restaurants are full/busy/do well/Tourists use the shops and restaurants.

GERMAN GENERAL READING 2008

1.
- 11(%) (They are on a diet)
- 28(%) (They don't feel like eating)
- 37(%) (It takes too much time)
- 24(%) (They are too lazy)

2.
- Luis (enjoyed the German hospitality)
- Kai (liked learning about German history)
- Pietro (enjoyed meeting other people)
- Natacha (was impressed by the cleanliness)

3.
- (50) Anyone who lights/has a cigarette/smokes will be fined/charged (£50)/ The fine/charge for lighting/having a cigarette/smoking
- (13 000) Scots/Scottish people/women and men die each/every/a year/died this/last year through/from/of smoking/it
- (5 000) (It is hoped that) (5 000) lives/people are/will/would be/will have been saved/rescued each/a/every year/yearly/annually (through the ban)/ (5 000) lives less will be lost each/a/every year.
- (2 500) (Critics fear that 2 500) jobs will be lost/People (fear they) will/are going to lose their jobs/Critics fear that (2 500) jobs are lost/Fear of job losses.

4.
- (Thomas)
  What went wrong
  There was/is a fire/flames in the hotel/Fire broke out in the hotel/His wife saw a fire in the hotel
  How it was solved
  His wife (saw the flames and) called/phoned/ contacted the fire brigade (in time)
- (Louisa)
  What went wrong
  Someone stole/took her (suit)case/bag/(hand) luggage (at the train station)
  How it was solved
  She was insured/had (travel) insurance/The insurance paid out (quickly)/covered it
- (Sandra)
  What went wrong
  She had an accident on a moped/She hired a moped and had an accident/She fell off a moped/She broke her leg(s)
  How it was solved
  (A)/(the) (nice) family helped her/me/(A)/(the) (nice) family took her/me to (a) doctor.

5. (*a*) He wanted to move/go/was moving/going/ moved/went/was returning/returned (back) to Hamburg/He had to go to Hamburg

(*b*) *Any two of:*
- He has worked there/here for 10 years
- He knows/knew (all) the customers/guests (well)
- He lives in the neighbourhood/area/near the bar/nearby
- It was a chance to/he had always wanted to/he could be/he is his own boss

(*c*)
- (His wife wants to) (serve/do/have) warm/hot food/meal(s)
- (Have a) beer garden behind the pub/bar/Have a beer garden in the summer

6.
- Lukas (finds it expensive but useful)
- Stefanie (chose it because of the colour)
- Ashraf (likes fastening it to their clothes)
- Lena (finds it easy to use)

7.
- D (Mechanic)
- E (Architect)
- C (Footballer)
- B (Actor)
- A (Chef)

8. (*a*) Ticks at:
- Box 2 (Plant a hedge)
- Box 4 (Keep the feeding area clean)
- Box 5 (Don't put salty food out)

(*b*) They feed (themselves and their young) on caterpillars and snails/They/the young eat/kill caterpillars and snails/To get rid of caterpillars and snails/It stops caterpillars and snails from destroying garden/They keep caterpillars and snails away

GERMAN GENERAL LISTENING 2008

1. There's lots for tourists (to see)/There's lots (for tourists) to see/There's lots of/many attractions

2. Ticks at:
   - Box 1 – (How long have you been learning German?)
   - Box 4 – (What do you do in your spare time?)
   - Box 6 – (What kind of music do you like?)

3. • (a) school (group)/(class)
   - (youth) hostel

4. Ticks at:
   - Box 2 – (Walking in the mountains).
   - Box 3 – (Castles).
   - Box 5 – (Riding school).

5. Tick at:
   Box 3 – (Ferry).

6. • The (flight) prices were/are (too) high/It was/is (too) expensive/It cost(s) too much/a lot/It isn't/ wasn't cheap/Too much money/Price(s)/They didn't have enough money
   - They/he had too much/a lot of luggage/They packed too many/a lot of items/They couldn't pack/take a lot

7. (In Scotland) (most/lots of) the shops are open on Sundays/In Germany, the shops are not/ hardly ever/mostly not open on Sundays

8. *Any two of:*
   - It tasted/was good/He liked/enjoyed it/It was delicious/tasty
   - It has (a lot of)/is full of fat/fatty/(too) fattening/It is not healthy/not good for you/It made him feel unhealthy
   - You shouldn't/couldn't/wouldn't eat it every day

9. (*a*) Tick at:
   Box 1 – (Romantic film)
   (*b*) 3 days ago/before

10. • He didn't sleep (well) (last night)/He had a bad sleep/He didn't get a good sleep/much sleep
    - He has a sore head/headache

11. • Sit/relax on the terrace/patio/deck/decking/Sit/ relax in the garden(s)/Go into/visit the garden(s)
    - Discuss/speak about/make plans/plan for next week/the week (ahead)/Discuss what to do next week

12. • (Most are quite/very/extremely) strict
    - They no longer/don't treat/handle/deal with them like (small) children/They treat them like adults

13. (*a*) Ticks at:
    - Box 2 – (To improve her language skills)
    - Box 4 – (To gain work experience)

    (*b*) A colleague(s) of her father/dad

GERMAN CREDIT READING 2008

1. (*a*) • (Many) (theatre) group(s) (in the town)/they/it were/was for teenagers/people/(young) children aged 13 or 14/13–14/13 or 14/13–14 year olds/Many were for 13 or 14/13–14 year olds
   - (Other) group(s)/they/it were/was (too) far away/on the outskirts/edge of town/too far from the town centre/It was (too) far to travel

   (*b*) She placed/put an advert/notice/advertised in the (regional/local) (news)paper (with the help of her parents)

   (*c*) In the first week over/more than 30 children registered/joined/wanted to join/turned up/volunteered/were there/In the first week she had over/more than 30 children

   (*d*) • Where/how will we/they/I/she find a director/producer/someone to direct/produce (for the show)?/Who will we find to direct/produce?/ She would have to find a director/producer
   - Will/would we/they be able to/can/could we/they rent/hire/use/get the/a/an school hall/assembly hall

   (*e*) • (On the first evening) the lights/spotlights/spots/floodlights/floods/footlights/light bulbs broke/went kaputt/didn't work/went out
   - (On the second evening) the main/lead(ing) actor/male lead/leading star had tonsillitis/a sore throat/was (so) hoarse (you could hardly hear him)

2. (*a*) To build/have/give/for (healthy) (self-) confidence/(self-)esteem/They will have no (self-) confidence

   (*b*) • Buy/wear the same clothes/follow the same fashion (as their friend(s)/the group)/ Buy/wear the clothes/the fashion of their friend(s)/the group
   - Neglect/don't do/don't care about their homework

   (*c*) • (Some) fight/row/argue/have arguments/hassle/aggro/fall out with their parents/yell at their parents
   - (Others) hide away/spend time/stay in/creep into their room/Spend (a lot of) time alone/on their own

   (*d*) *Any three of:*
   - Be a friend and less like a parent/less parenty
   - Discuss (everything)/communicate with/talk/ speak to their teenager/them
   - Take their teenager/them/their problem(s) seriously
   - Treat/speak to/deal with their teenager/them like an adult/grown-up

   (*e*) When she spends (all) her (pocket) money in one day/on the day she gets it/when she runs out of pocket money in one day

   (*f*) She is hardly ever/never/seldom/rarely at home/at the house/She is not at home enough/for long (periods of time)/She is always out

3. (*a*) • (More) variety
   - (Frequent) contact with (other) people/person/human(s)

   (*b*) (For many people) (a high) salary/money/wage is not (very) important/doesn't matter/doesn't play a big role

   (*c*) *Any one of:*
   - Describe/make up/formulate/(write a) description of the/your ideal job
   - Consider/think about/look for (possible) alternative(s)

   (*d*) *Any two of:*
   - Describe/make up/formulate/write a description of the/your ideal job
   - Consider/think about (possible) alternative(s)

- Do it at/during a quiet/free/peaceful/calm time/hour/moment/when it's quiet/Be quiet/at peace for an hour
- Don't think about/consider it for (too) long/Don't spend a long time thinking/Don't take (too) long over it
- Write down ideas quickly/spontaneously

(*e*)
- (What are) the worst (working) conditions/ circumstances (you can imagine)?
- With which colleagues/people could/can you not work (under any circumstances)?/ Who could/can you not work with?/With which colleagues would you not like to work?

GERMAN CREDIT LISTENING 2008

1. (*a*) She earns (quite) a lot of/(quite) good money/It pays (quite) well/The/her money/wage/salary/pay/ What she earns/The pay is okay/not bad.

(*b*) *Any two of:*
- She/he argues/fights/rows with/shouts at the customers/people.
- She/he is (often very) impolite/unpolite/rude/ cheeky.
- She/he has no (new) ideas/plans for the café/how to improve the café/make the café better

2. *Any three of:*
- The café is (too) dark/dull/Make it less dark/dull/brighter/lighter/Have white/light (-coloured) curtains/Brighten up the café
- (Have/provide a) better selection of/ better/more magazines/(news)papers/ (Have/provide) magazines and (news)papers/She would like the customers to read newspapers and magazines
- (Introduce/serve/sell) (new) dishes/food from Italy or/and France/(Have a) French or/and Italian theme on the menu/for food/Change the food to Italian or/and French
- Make the menu/food (more) interesting/exciting/Make it more interesting/exciting

3.
- To finance/pay for/fund her studies/schooling/ education/To cover student finances/fees/To pay student bills/for being a student/her education/Needs money for her student fund/Earn money for college/university/She is a student and needs the money
- Her father/dad is unemployed/jobless/doesn't work/have a job/Her father/dad cannot/is not able to support her (financially)/give her money

4.
- You need/(can) have time for/to/you/yourself/on your own/alone/time to do what you want
- (You can) meet/see/spend time with friends/ people outwith/out of/outside/after school

5. *Any two of:*
- There's not enough/no space/room/place (for the pupils)/The place/it is not big enough/It is (too) crowded
- The (class)room(s)/class(es)/are/is (too) small(er)/(more) narrow/cramped/squashed/ tight/compact/crowded/are not big
- The bike stand(s)/bike shed(s)/bike rack(s)/bike shelter(s) are/is at the other end of the playground/school (yard)/The bike stand(s)/bike shed(s)/bike rack(s)/bike shelter(s) are/is no longer/not at the entrance/The bike stand(s)/bike shed(s)/bike rack(s)/bike shelter(s) are/is (too) far away

6. *Any two of:*
- It was (a) historic (building)/It was made of (red) brick(s)/It was red
- It/the building/the school looked/was (much) nice(r)/prettier/pretty/(more) beautiful/It etc was (much) better-looking/The look of the building etc.
- (The classrooms/school/it were/was) cool(er)/cold(er) in summer

7. (*a*)
- Free (entry)/it doesn't cost anything/no charge for pupils/school kids/school children/students
- (Last year) she read (an interesting article) about the/a/an artist/painter/there was an (interesting) article about the/a/an artist/painter

(*b*) He came from Russia (to Austria)/He came (to Austria) in 1975/He came to Austria

8. • He will (help his friend to) collect/get/buy/pick up (a) drink(s)/juice for his/a party (from the supermarket)
   • He has/they have to pick up/meet/collect friend(s)/people at/from the station/the train

9. • Tinned/ready-made/supermarket/bought/purchased/packet soup contains/has fewer/less vitamins (than home-made soup/it/her soup)/ Home-made soup/it/her soup contains/has more vitamins (than tinned/ready-made/supermarket/ bought/purchased/packet soup)/Home-made soup/it/her soup contains/has lots of/many vitamins
   • (She uses) (fresh) vegetable(s) from the garden/ She has grown her own vegetables/Fresh vegetable(s) taste(s)/are good
   • It will be ready/prepared/on the table in/it takes half an hour/30 minutes/She can make it in half an hour/30 minutes

10. *Any three of:*
   • They work during their lunch/dinner break/at lunchtime/dinner time at midday/They eat little/nothing at lunchtime/dinner time/They don't have a proper lunch/dinner/They have no time to eat at lunchtime/dinner time/They never eat at lunchtime/dinner time
   • They are (so) tired at night/in the evening/after work
   • They cannot be bothered cooking (anything) (proper)/They don't cook (anything)/It's no fun cooking/They can't cook
   • They get/eat something from the snack bar/take away/fast food/They go to the snack bar/take- away/They order in/phone for food

GERMAN GENERAL READING 2009

1. (*a*) • More/a lot of space/room/(A) big(ger) area(s)/big(ger)
   • Better/good sports facilities/possibilities/opportunities/equipment/Better/improved (for) sport(s)

   (*b*) • It's (a)/(an) ugly/horrible/nasty looking (building)/(There's) (too much) concrete/It's made of concrete

2. | | |
   |---|---|
   | (Entertainment for teenagers) | Positive |
   | (Shops) | Negative |
   | (Litter) | Negative |

3. (*a*) *Any two of:*
   • Every Saturday/On Saturday(s) there is a film programme (for them/children)/(a) (children's) film(s)
   • Before the film, the children can play (together)
   • The film(s) are/is short/not too long
   • The film(s) are/is (suitable/ideal) for children/them/It's children's films

   (*b*) *Any one of:*
   • There are films on for them/adults/parents at the same time/They/adults/parents can watch a film at the same time
   • They can watch a film for free/for nothing/at no extra cost/charge
   • They can watch/see a film/go to cinema without (having to get) a babysitter

4. (*a*) • (If you spend your holidays) at/by/near the sea/At/by/near the seaside/beach/if there is a sea
   • Go to the chemist/pharmacy/pharmacist/Go to the/a/your doctor

   (*b*) • Box 2 (Airports)

5. (*a*) • When people/passengers are impolite/rude/cheeky/give him cheek

   (*b*) *Any two of:*
   • Makes sure that (all) cars get on board (safely)/ Gets the cars on board/Helps the cars on board/ Supervises the cars going on board/Makes sure the cars are safely on board/Guides/puts cars on board
   • Checks that (all) passengers have a (valid) ticket/travel card/boarding card/Examines the tickets
   • Paints (the boat/ferry/it)

6. (*a*) • You can avoid traffic/jams/blockages/congestion
   • You can stay slim/thin/slender/skinny/It makes you slim(mer)/thin(ner)/It keeps you slim/thin

   (*b*) • On their way to work/In the rush hour/In/at busy/peak/main/prime (traffic) time(s)/When the roads are busy/In busy traffic/When it's busy

   (*c*) • They are (too)/(very) narrow/It's a tight space/ They're not wide enough

7. | | |
   |---|---|
   | (the accommodation) | Frank |
   | (the scenery) | Anna |
   | (the people they stayed with) | Max |
   | (the food) | Selassi |

8. | | |
   |---|---|
   | (It doesn't matter if others do better than you) | Julia |
   | (Organise your work area) | Karla |
   | (Don't study after having a meal) | Vadim |

9. (Nina likes watching sport on TV) False
(Axel finds watching TV relaxing) True
(Andreas is allowed to watch TV whenever he wants) False

10. (*a*) • It becomes/is a meeting point/place/destination/travel spot for people/human beings/crowds from all over the world/around the world/People come from all over the world/It's a target for people from all over the world/It attracts people from all over the world

(*b*) • Television/TV tower

(*c*) • From a boat/ship/On the/going up/down the river/Rhein/Rhine

GERMAN GENERAL LISTENING 2009

1. (*a*) (They go to Majorca every year.) True
(They arrived yesterday.) False

(*b*) • Is this your first time/year in Majorca/here/there?/Have you been to Majorca/here/there before?

2. • A/the train (journey/ride/fare/pass/ticket) in/around Germany/Travelling by train

3. • They met there (for the first time 20 years ago).

4. *Any three of:*
- The water/sea is clear/blue/light blue
- (It/the beach/the sand is very) clean/tidy
- Quiet/peaceful/not crowded/not busy
- You must/should go

5. (*a*) • Box 1 – There is a big choice.
• Box 3 – The food is cheap.

(*b*) • vegetarian/vegetable(s)/veggie

6. (*a*) • Box 3 – At the harbour

(*b*) • meat (dishes)

7. *Any two of:*
- She stayed/lay/was/sat in the sun too long/a long time/She spent too long in the sun/She sunbathed too long/a long time.
- She fell asleep.
- She got sunburn/sunstroke/heatstroke/She got burnt/burns.

8. • Use/wear/apply/put on/get/buy (a good/high factor)(sun)cream/lotion/spray/block/screen

• Wear a (sun) hat/cap/something to protect/cover your head

• Stay under a parasol/(sun) umbrella/in the shade/Go in(to) the shade/Stay shaded

9. (*a*) • Box 1 – (Presents)

(*b*) • (till) late (in the evening)/in (to) the evening/at night/late (at) night/till the evening/all evening
• helpful

10. • (rent for/to hire) student/university/college flat/accommodation/residence/home/house/room/apartment/place/Student rent

11. *Any two of:*
- (hundreds of old sailing) boats/ships
- firework(s)
- Spanish dancing/dancers/dance (in the town hall square)/You can do Spanish dancing

12. (*a*) • Box 3 – (single bed, wardrobe, TV.)

(*b*) • She/you can't open the window/The window doesn't open/The window is stuck.

GERMAN CREDIT READING 2009

1. (*a*) • Time for recovery/Time to/they can recover/relax/rest/recuperate (after the strain of a long school year)/Relaxing/It's the end of a long/hard school year.
 • Possible to/opportunity to/you can spend time/spend longer/hang about with/see/meet up with friends/relatives/family/A long break with friends/relatives/family.

 (*b*) • How to/they have to occupy their child/children/kids/keep their child busy/what to do with their child/What can their child do/They have nothing to keep their child occupied.

 (*c*) • When the weather is bad/temperature(s) are/is low/cold/bad/when it's cold.

 (*d*) • They spend too much/a lot of/a long time in front of a screen/computer/TV (already)/(anyway)/
 They are/sit in front of a screen/computer/TV often/all the time (already)/(anyway)/They play them a lot (already)/(anyway).

 (*e*) • They enjoy/get/have (the undivided) attention (of their parents).
 • They (need to) feel important/valued.

2. (*a*) • (The risk of) alcohol poisoning (is high.)/It poisons them/you/It's poisonous
 • They cannot take/stand/tolerate/handle as much alcohol/it (as adults)/They cannot take/stand/tolerate/handle alcohol/it as much/as well/so well/like adults (can)/They are not as resistant/Their tolerance is lower/less/Adults can handle alcohol/it/It takes less alcohol to do it.

 (*b*) • They don't want to be an outsider/excluded from the group/They want to fit in/don't want to be left out/They want to be in/belong to a group/They are an outsider if they don't drink/They want to do the same as their friends.
 • (Because of/they suffer from/to drive away) loneliness/solitude/(They are) lonely/They don't want to be lonely.

 (*c*) *Any two of:*
 • His parents got divorced/separated/split up.
 • To escape from/stop/get rid of/forget about his worries/troubles/problems/He was worried/To make his worries etc disappear/go away.
 • It made the/his world/life/it/bearable/tolerable/He found the world/life/it unbearable (without alcohol)/It allowed him to cope

 (*d*) • His marks/grades/work/standards/were/was getting worse/slipping/bad/not the same/down (a level/grade)/dropping/lower/poorer

 (*e*) • They never discussed/couldn't discuss family problem(s)/problem(s) the family had (with him).

 (*f*) • He recognised the problem(s) from his own experience/His brother drank (too much/a lot)/had the same problem/had a drink(ing) problem (when he was young/younger)/His brother got drunk a lot/all the time/He had experience of this problem/situation with his brother/He had the same/similar problem/situation with his brother/His brother was an alcoholic.

 (*g*) • (He knows) he/she is (always) there (for him)/helps him/supports him/speaks to him/gives him advice in a crisis/when there is a problem/
 He can go to him/her/phone him/her in a crisis/when there is a problem.

3. (*a*) • It is boom time/a busy time/peak time/Great demand/In demand/Lots of people need a taxi/You can earn a lot/good money/It pays well.

 (*b*) • (That) you know your way around the town/area/city/Hamburg/You have a good knowledge of the town etc/You know (about) the town etc/You are familiar with the town etc/You know where the streets are.

 (*c*) • Ten/10 hours/10-hour shift (in a car) requires a lot of stamina/staying power/endurance.

 (*d*) • He is (a) sociable (person)/His nature is to socialise.
 • He had hardly any/no opportunity to/he couldn't chat/talk to his colleagues/co-workers (and he couldn't stand that).

 (*e*) • His brother-in-law was selling/had to sell his firm/taxi (because he was moving to Frankfurt)/He (and his wife) borrowed money from people he knew/acquaintances/friends.

 (*f*) • (He/they wanted) to propose (to a woman/partner/girlfriend/wife from there)/Make a proposal to a woman/partner/girlfriend/wife/ He/they had fallen/was in love with a woman from there.

 (*g*) *Any two of:*
 • Had/went for something to eat/dinner
 • Went to/stayed in a hotel.
 • Rested/slept for two days/Took two days off (work)/to himself/a two-day break.
 • Promised/swore to himself/said that he would never do it/the trip again.

GERMAN CREDIT LISTENING 2009

1. (*a*) • (All her) colleagues/workmates/people/everyone (at work)/are/is (very) nice/pleasant.

• She gets (10%) discount (on trips/holidays/journeys)/ She gets 10%/money off (trips/holidays/journeys).

(*b*) • She has to work/works 6 days a week/out of 7.

2. • The doctor recommended it/advised/told her to/said/It is (much) healthier/healthy/It keeps you/her healthy/It is good/better for your/her health
• It is better/good for/helps/saves the environment/world/planet/earth.
• She/it saves money/It costs less/It doesn't cost as much/It's cheap(er)/Driving is (more) expensive/Petrol/fuel is expensive/petrol/fuel costs are high.

3. • There were/he met authors from (more than) 20 countries/of (more than) 20 nationalities.

• You could speak/talk to/interview the author(s)/ask the author(s) questions/things/You could speak/talk to/interview them/ask them questions/things

4. *Any two of:*
• He is interested in/likes war films/It is a war film.
• He read/saw (a) review(s)/write-up(s)/He read/saw it in the (news)paper.
• It's (supposed to be) exciting.

5. *Any two of:*
• He has spent/is spending/spends/too much/a lot of/(all) his/the money this week (already).
• It is (high) time he spent an evening/stayed at home/in (the house)/He should/she wants him to spend an evening/night/stay at home/in (the house).
• He should/has to (make time to) tidy/clean/do/organise his (bed) room/He has not tidied/cleaned/organised his room/His room is untidy.

6. • She (constantly) forgets homework/She doesn't do/never does/brings in/hands in homework.
• She is (often very) cheeky/rude/impolite (when she speaks) (to teachers)/she talks back.
• (Last week) she stole/took a teacher's (hand)bag.

7. (*a*) • They worked/had a job PLUS ONE OF holiday/bakery/when they were young.

(*b*) *Any two of:*
• Her brother emigrated/moved to/is in/lives in America/She misses her brother.
• They had to sell the house.
• Her mother lost her job/doesn't have a job/is unemployed/is not working

8. (*a*) • Teacher(s)/school have/has tried/offer(ed) to help/help(ed) her but she won't listen/she doesn't want it.

(*b*) • There are others with (bigger) problems/There are bigger/other problems than hers/She's not the only one with problems.

• Others/the class/others in the class want to learn/(She has to) allow others to learn/Let others learn/She's stopping others/him from learning/Others are entitled to an education.

9. *Any two of:*
• She didn't have a mobile phone/her own phone (to speak to friends)/There were no mobile phones.
• (Her dad complained that) the phone bill was high/expensive/Her dad complained about the phone bill.
• You couldn't see (the latest) (a) film(s) at home/You could only see (the latest) film(s) at the cinema/You had to see (the latest) (a) film(s) at the cinema.

10. • They have to wear/have the right clothes/They have to wear clothes to be/that are in/in fashion/in trend/cool/popular/fashionable/accepted.

• It is difficult/hard to/you can't find/get a (good) job/work when you leave school/after school.

GERMAN GENERAL READING 2010

1. (*a*) • (In a) good mood/temper/In/at the factory
- Employing/hiring/finding/placing (new) workers/giving (new) jobs/filling work places/interviewing (people for jobs)

(*b*) • Work shift(s)/do shift work (patterns)
- Travel/go abroad/to different countries/(Do) business/sell/work abroad/in different countries

2. (*a*) • (He) saw/watched/went to/(was) at/a (seven-a-side) tournament/it/rugby/a rugby team in Scotland

(*b*) *Any two of:*
- Every/each/a game/it lasts/you play (only) fourteen minutes
- You can have/watch a (whole) tournament in one/a day
- You save overnight/accommodation costs (for teams)

3. • Hamit (finds out about local history)
- Ruth (spends time tidying up)
- Ruth (likes not having to spend money)
- Thomas (writes and illustrates poems)

4. (*a*) • In an old folks'/people's/OAP/retirement home

(*b*) • Check/test/examine the fire alarm/make sure the fire alarm works

(*c*) • Close/shut/lock/fasten (all) the window(s)

(*d*) • (He meets/met/helps/talks to/works with) (so many) nice young people/children/kids/pupils

5. • The water/it is polluted/dirty/(of) pollution
- (In/at the) river
- It's (too) far (away)

6. • Lars (would prefer to go away for Christmas)
- Sabrina (finds some members of their family too loud)
- Heike (doesn't like the town being busy)
- Sabrina (thinks about poverty and war)

7. (*a*) • (They have lovely children's) furniture/ Furniture is suitable/the right height for children

(*b*) • They have (fairytale)/(romantic) figures/ characters/Hansel/Gretel/fairytale creatures/fairytales on them/to do with fairytales

(*c*) *Any one of:*
- Next door/Next to/beside the child's room/ through a wall
- Through a (connecting) door/through to the next room/There's a connection through

(*d*) *Any one of:*
- It has a connecting door/It is connected to the child's room/It has a connection to the child's room/The rooms are connected
- (It is) roomy/spacious/large/big
- (You have a great) view of the sea/You can see the sea

8. • False (Oya can speak to her parents about everything)
- True (Her mum is more understanding than her dad)
- True (She would like to have children one day)

9. (*a*) • She was on a school trip/With the school

(*b*) *Any one of:*
- She saw (lots of) (new) plants/flowers (in Japan)/ She liked the plants/flowers/The plants/flowers were beautiful
- Exchange family's dad/Herr/Mr Tashiguro/the dad was a (keen) gardener

(*c*) *Any one of:*
- They don't have/there's not a lot of space/room/ They have a small(er) garden/don't have a big (enough) garden
- The weather/it is/was (too) damp/wet/wetter (in Germany) (for exotic plants)/The weather is/was not suitable/not good for the plants/exotic plants/Japanese plants

GERMAN GENERAL LISTENING 2010

1. • Box 1 – Where do you come from?
• Box 3 – How long are you staying in Germany?

2. • Box 1 – ice skating
• Box 3 – boat trip
• Box 6 – bowling

3. • A teacher (in her school)/her teacher worked/lived in France/A teacher (in her school)/her teacher has friend(s) in France/A/her teacher went to/was in France for two years/spent two years in France
• A/her teacher gave her an/the/her address.
If teacher mentioned in first bullet point, it is not required in second bullet point.

4. • In a (small) village.
• Next to/near/beside a church.

5. • You learn/find out/she has learned (a lot) about another/their country/other countries/abroad.
• Getting/receiving letters (is fun/exciting)/(She likes) getting/receiving letters.

6. • She (and her parents) moved to/was/were in/lived in a new/different/another/strange town(s)/city/cities.
• She had no friend(s)/They were her only friends.

7. • Bottom left box.

8. • Box 2 – He didn't get on with the family in Scotland.
• Box 3 – He had sore ears.
• Box 6 – He couldn't find his passport.

9. (*a*) • On the last day of the month/At the end of the month.

(*b*) • He has to/needs to buy/buys (his own) clothes.
• (All his) friend(s)/everyone get(s) (a lot) more than him.

10. (*a*) • Box 2 – watch.

(*b*) • Box 3 – €165.

11. (*a*) • Chemist(s)/pharmacy/apothecary.

(*b*) • Everything/it is (too) expensive/dear.

12. (*a*) • Quiet/peaceful/calm.

(*b*) • Box 1 – There is no traffic.

GERMAN CREDIT READING 2010

1. (*a*) • She has/they have never/not learned/she doesn't/cannot speak (foreign) language(s) properly/right/well/correctly/She has never really learned (foreign) language(s)

(*b*) • They want to be/are/feel independent/So they are (more) independent/have (more) independence
• They want to (learn to) make their own decisions/learn from their own decisions

(*c*) • These/youth travel firms/they choose leader(s)/guide(s)/courier(s) carefully
• You can contact them/the leader(s)/guide(s) at any time/hour/round the clock/24/7/They are available/within reach at any time/round the clock/24/7/You can always contact them/They are always available

(*d*) • Is the (travel)/(tour) organiser/agent/operator/firm/company well known/famous/familiar?
• What/how many safety/security precautions/ measures are there?/(Are there) safety/security (measures/precautions)?/What is the safety/ security like?/Is there anything for her safety/ security?/Is it safe?

2. (*a*) *Any one of:*
• (There is so much) rubbish/litter/trash
• There are hardly any/not a lot of/no visitors/ No-one/nobody visits/goes/comes

(*b*) *Any two of:*
• He grew up in the town
• Park was (an important) part of his childhood/life as a child/He has memories (of it) from his childhood/when he was a child
• He used to feed/fed animals there/He used to go/ went there with his parents (almost) every weekend/at the weekend

(*c*) *Any two of:*
• The/a (first) (rubbish) bin(s)/basket(s)/ bucket(s)/was empty/The contents of (a) bin(s)/basket(s)/bucket(s)/were everywhere/all over the place
• (Empty) plastic bottle(s) under (a) bench(es)/ seat(s)
• (Drinks) can(s) on/in the grass

(*d*) • Racing dogs/(Racing) dogs run/running/race/ racing (around)/(Racing) dogs disturb/disturbing the peace/quiet(ness)
• Children/people are injured/hurt/cut/harmed by (shards/pieces of) glass (on the grass)

(*e*) • (Visitors must) keep/put dogs/pets on a leash/lead
• There is/are/install(ed) CCTV/video surveillance/(video) cameras (in the park)/Videos are taken to keep an eye on it/the park
• Pupils/schools clear up/clean up/tidy up (rubbish) twice a month

3. (*a*) *Any one of:*
• The best players are (world) famous/They want to be (world) famous
• You can make a fortune/a lot of money/become rich/Good pay

(*b*) • He got a three-year contract/deal/He got a junior contract/deal/He got a contract/deal at 17/He was signed for three years/as a junior/at 17

(*c*) • A (heavy) tool box/tool crate fell on his (left) foot

(*d*) • He wanted to avoid/avoided (contact with other) people
• He didn't want to speak/talk/wasn't speaking/ talking about his (football) career

(*e*) *Any one of:*
• He didn't work hard/wasn't hardworking/didn't try at school/He didn't study enough
• He left school without/with no qualifications/(a) certificate

(*f*) • (The proper/right/good) education/training is (very) important
• How to/he can write/fill out/complete an application (form) (for a job)
• How to make/give/leave/he made a positive/ good impression at (an) interview

GERMAN CREDIT LISTENING 2010

1. (*a*) *Any one of:*
• His mum works/worked (full time/all day).
• He didn't want to/fancy/choose/couldn't be bothered to stay at home/in the house/alone/by himself/on his own.

(*b*) • He met/there were (lots of other) young people/ people his age/youths/teenagers/(older) children (his age)/friends his age.
• There was a full/busy programme (every day)/ (Every day was) full of activities/lots of activities/ (There was) lots to do.

2. • Bike/cycle tour/ride/run/cycling (and saw the area).
• Visited/went to a/stayed at farm/farmhouse.
• (Tried/did) water sport(s).

3. (*a*) • His dad got/was offered a job/works/abroad/in a foreign/different country.

(*b*) • He has (important) exams (next year).

4. (*a*) • For pupils who don't want to/are scared to discuss/talk about problems/things with/talk to a teacher(s)/For pupils who have problems talking to a teacher(s).

(*b*) • Pupils write their problems (and feelings) in/send an e-mail (and they get a reply a few days later)/ (Through) e-mail.

5. (*a*) • The head teacher/rector/school director spoke about it/was/advertised it on TV/television.
• (Two) pupils/children (from his class)/his/a/the class wrote an article for/advertised it in/wrote about it for the newspaper.

(*b*) • More than 40 schools (in the region/area) have (brought in) the scheme/system/it.

6. • He/she has to work in the summer/in the holidays/He has to work when most/other people are on holiday/He doesn't get summer holidays/They can't go on holiday because he has to work.
• He is (often) (very) tired (when he gets home)/It is tiring.

7. • You can earn a lot (of money)/decent/good money/It is well paid.
• You can (often) eat free (of charge) (in the hotel)/You get free meals/food/lunch etc.

8. (*a*) • South(ern) Europe.

(*b*) • *Any two of:*
• Laze around/be lazy/relax.
• Forget about stress/work/De-stress/Release stress.
• Go on excursions/trips/outings/tours/Visit places.

9. *Any two of*
• They/we (have to) visit the sights/go sightseeing (and that doesn't interest him)/He's not interested in (visiting) the sights/sightseeing.
• His parents/they don't (want to) go out/do anything at night/in the evening/enjoy the nightlife/He wants to/he's not allowed to go out at night/in the evening/enjoy the nightlife.
• They/we (have to) stay in (the hotel) in the evening/ at night.

10. *Any three of:*
• (He says) granny/she can cook better/is a better cook (than her/his mum/his parents).

- He knows (lots of) young people/youths/teenagers/children/(There are) (lots of) young people/youths/teenagers/children near/nearby/close by/not far away/round about.
- He won't get bored/It won't be boring.
- He can (help grandad to) mow/maintain/cut the lawn/grass.

GERMAN GENERAL READING 2011

1. • Amelie
   • Jessica
   • Nico

2. • Smart/stylish/chic/classy
   • (Silver) name badge/tag/sign/label/plate/ Badge/tag/sign/label/plate with name on it
   • No one breaks/damages/smashes anything/ artwork/paintings/Nothing is broken/ damaged/smashed

3. (*a*) *Any two of:*
   - (They are) worried/anxious/scared/ nervous/stressed about/fear of the (new) school year
   - (They want/will get) better/to improve grade(s)/mark(s)/result(s)
   - They get bored (during the holidays)/ Holidays are boring/You don't get bored

   (*b*) • How to manage/use/deal with/spend time (better)/How to make time (more) useful
   • (It's important to/how to) discuss/talk about problem(s)

4. (*a*) *Any two of:*
   - (They have the same/similar/identical) (hand)writing
   - They use/say the same words/say the same things/The things they say/the words they use/say
   - (They have the same) taste(s) (in many things)/They like the same things

   (*b*) *Any one of:*
   - Her dad/father has (found) a (new) job/post/position/ place of work/workplace/work placement/Her dad's job etc
   - Her new house is far away

   (*c*) • Jana/she/it/Jana's/her (new) house is/will be (so) far away

5. • **Box 2** – Jana will have to make new friends
   • **Box 3** – You can visit Jana in the holidays
   • **Box 6** – You should think about the future

6. (*a*) • Do less/fewer than two hours/lessons sport/PE in a (normal)/per week/Do two hours or less sport/PE per week
   • Eat enough vegetables/veg
   • Eat (at least) two portions/pieces of fruit per/a day

   (*b*) • She has banned/got rid of/stopped (serving) unhealthy food/junk food/unhealthy eating/ Unhealthy food/junk food/unhealthy eating is banned/forbidden/not allowed

7. • True
   • False
   • True
   • False

8. • **Karla**
   Switch(es)/Turn(s) off electronic/electrical equipment/things/ devices/appliances/electricals/electronics/everything before (going to) bed/when they are in bed/at bedtime
   • **Sahiba**
   (Her dad) switch(es)/turn(s) off the car/engine/ motor/stops the engine/motor (if they wait for long) at lights
   • **Andi**
   Has a shower/Don't have a bath (tub) (in the house)/Don't/doesn't take a bath

- **Irfan**
  Only use(s) the dishwasher when it's (really) full/Fill(s) up the dishwasher

9. • **Box 2** – All meals
   • **Box 3** – Insurance
   • **Box 6** – Walks after dark

GERMAN GENERAL LISTENING 2011

1. • (Doing/has) homework
   • Walking/exercising dog(s)

2. • Baker(s)/bakery/bakers shop
   • Hairdresser(s)/Salon

3. • **Box 1** – Are you tired?
   • **Box 2** – Are you thirsty?

4. (*a*) • (Going to/appointment at) dentist/Appointment for teeth/orthodontist

   (*b*) • Barbecue/BBQ (party)
   • (You/he/she will) get to know/meet (David's/his) friend(s)/He/David will introduce his friend(s)

5. *Any two of:*
   • In the town hall/town house/city hall
   • Young people get two (tickets) for the price of one/buy one (ticket) get one free/
   People under 16/under 16s get two (tickets) for the price of one/buy one (ticket) get one free
   • Do you want to go?/Asks if you want to go

6. (*a*) • **Box 2** – tram

   (*b*) • (BUS) Have to wait (a long time)/He doesn't like waiting
   • (TAXI) Expensive/Costs a lot/too much/more/Too much money/The cost

7. • Straight/Straightened
   • Glasses/spectacles/specs/Skirt
   • (Short) skirt

8. • **Box 2** – in a bad mood
   • **Box 4** – impolite

9. • One and a half years/A year and a half/18 months/1.5 years
   • Two/2 (young/small/smaller) daughter(s)/girl(s)

10. • Can explain/explains (things) (well)/Good at explaining/Good explainer/He makes things clear/He is clear/a clear teacher/ He teaches (things) clearly
    • Organises/organised/arranges/arranged trip(s)/excursion(s)/outing(s) day(s) out (for the class)

11. (*a*) • **Box 3** – Highland scenery

    (*b*) • It rained (whole time)/(The) rain

12. • Stomach/tummy/belly ache/pains/Sore stomach/tummy/belly/Stomach/tummy bug

GERMAN CREDIT READING 2011

1. (*a*) • (Almost) a quarter (of all students) took/take/had/have/did/have done a gap year/it/that (last year)

(*b*) • (You have time) to relax/rest/recover/chill after/from (the) exams
• (A chance to experience a great/big/large) adventure(s)/Adventurous experience(s)
• It's their first experience of work/work experience/job/They had/have no/little time for a (part-time) job while in/at school

(*c*) *Any two of:*
• (Work(ing) in an) old folk's/senior citizen's/retirement/elderly/nursing/care home (in Peru)
• Pick(ing)/gather(ing)/harvest(ing)/pluck(ing) fruit (in Canada)
• (Work(ing) in a) school for disabled/handicapped (children/people) (in India)

(*d*) • (You need/it's difficult to get) a (work) permit/permission/visa

2. (*a*) • They were caught in/there was a (bad/heavy/hard) (thunder) storm/A (thunder) storm began/There was thunder and lightning
• They had to sleep/spend/stay/shelter for the night in a (small) village school

(*b*) *Any one of:*
• Cheap/affordable accommodation for young people/youngster(s)/youth(s)/teenager(s)
• Friendship/making friends/being friendly/friendliness and tolerance/being tolerant among/for/towards young people/youngster(s)/youth(s)/teenager(s)

(*c*) • The importance of the environment (in Germany)/The environment is important

(*d*) • A (special) stamp/coin are/is/were/was being released/issued/made/given out/launched/printed/unveiled/will be on sale/A new stamp/coin

(*e*) • Meet (young) people from other/different countries/lands/places/regions/parts (of Germany)/from all over (Germany/the world)/Meet foreign (young) people

(*f*) • They had to get/fetch water from a well/fountain/spring
• A/one swing/Only/nothing but swing(s) (in the garden)

(*g*) • She got to know/became familiar with the mountain(s)/hill(s) (for the first time)

3. (*a*) • (Mae/they) read/studied/bought (lots of/a travel/tourist) guide(s)/travel/tourist/guide book(s)/From (travel/tourist) guide(s)/travel/tourist/guide book(s)
• (Ferdia/they) studied/learned/read (about) the culture (of/in the country)

(*b*) • The car(s) was/were/is/are not (especially) reliable
• The roads/streets (in Russia) are not as/so good (as in Germany)/worse (than in Germany)

(*c*) *Any three of:*
• (There are so many/plague of) mosquitoes/midges/gnats/Lots of mosquito/midge/gnat/A mosquito/midge/gnat problem/Mosquito/midge/gnat bites
• (It's hard to) find/finding wood for a fire/firewood
• There are hardly any/not a lot of/not many/not a lot of/(almost) no shops
• You have to take (a lot of) food/groceries (on/in the canoe/with you)

(*d*) • The equipment/gear costs a lot (of money)/too much/The cost of the equipment/gear
• It costs too much/a lot/it's overpriced/the prices/costs are high to hire/rent a canoe/kayak/kajak/The cost of hiring/renting a canoe/kayak/kajak

(*e*) • You're not allowed to/so you won't disturb/ disrupt/scare off/it disturbs/disrupts/scares off the (water) birds

GERMAN CREDIT LISTENING 2011

1. (*a*) • Travel by train/rail/Go on a train/rail/trip/ride/tour/Travel/tour (around/in/across) Europe/go around Europe

(*b*) • (You have so much) freedom/(You are) free
• If one town/place/somewhere isn't nice/good you can go on/drive off to the next one/ somewhere else/you have the next town to look forward to

2. • The plane/it/they had to land/landed in France
• A(n)/the (old/elderly) man/person/someone was ill/sick/in pain
• They arrived/were five/5 hours late/later/They had a five/5-hour delay/were delayed by five/5 hours

3. (*a*) • (His firm is) opening/(has) opened a (new) office(s)/A new office(s)/He is working at/his firm is moving to a new office/A (new) office is being built

(*b*) • He has to buy/get/find furniture (for the office)

• He has to find/get (two new) secretaries/secretary

4. *Any two of:*
• They/she/we had to stay/stayed at home/in the house/didn't go away last summer/year
• Her mum/she works (full time/all day)
• Her mum/she needs/deserves/must have/would benefit from/requires/wants two weeks/fortnight (of) rest/relaxation/recovery/Her mum/she needs two weeks/fortnight of good weather

5. (*a*) • (He had the) 'flu

(*b*) *Any one of:*
• He has no/doesn't have any free time
• He has no/doesn't have any time for anything/things/activities/to himself/have fun
• He can't do other things/(other) activities/anything else
• It's taking (up) his free time

6. *Any three of:*
• She has learned/learns/can learn/wants to learn so much/a lot (from him/from his programmes)
• He makes everything/it (so) easy/simple/He makes everything/it look easy
• He has a (good) sense of humour
• His shows/programmes/episodes are (so) funny

7. (*a*) • Watch TV/it/things on their mobile(s)/phone(s)/Put TV shows on their mobile/phone

(*b*) • (They find) TV/it more important than (contact with) friend(s)/They prefer TV/it to friend(s)/They'd rather watch TV/it than contact/meet/go out with friend(s)

8. (*a*) • They play/do gigs in a pub(s)/bar(s)/club(s) (on Saturday evenings)

(*b*) • (They need/to buy) better/new instrument(s) (urgently)

9. (*a*) • 30(th) May

(*b*) • Helps (young) people/teenager(s)/youth(s)/children/kid(s) who (have to) sleep/live/stay on the street(s)/have nowhere to sleep/live/stay/homeless people etc/people etc who sleep rough/Prevents/doesn't let people sleep/live on the streets

10. • Selling tickets (before the concert)
• Serving/selling/handing out/giving out/getting/helping with drinks/refreshments/juice in the interval/break
• Tidying/packing/clearing/cleaning (up)(at the end)

Published by Bright Red Publishing Ltd, 6 Stafford Street, Edinburgh, EH3 7AU
Tel: 0131 220 5804, Fax: 0131 220 6710, enquiries: sales@brightredpublishing.co.uk,
www.brightredpublishing.co.uk

Official SQA answers to 978-1-84948-171-7
2007-2011